FOUNDATION COURSE IN ENGLISH FOR COMPUTING

CS-610

For

Bachelor In Computer Applications

Valid For

IGNOU, Vinayaka Mission University, IP University, Delhi University, CCS University, JMI University, B. M. V. Open University (KOTA), M. P. Bhoj Open University(M.P.), Tamilnadu Open University, YCM Open University (Maharashtra), Mahatma Gandhi University (Kottyam), M. D. University, and all other Indian Universities.

GPH BOOK™

GULLYBABA PUBLISHING HOUSE (P) Ltd.

AN ISO 9001:2008 CERTIFIED CO.

GullyBaba Publishing House (P) Ltd.
2525 / 193, Ist Floor, Onkar Nagar-A,
Tri Nagar, Delhi-110035
Ph: 9350849407, 9312235086, 011-27387998

E-mail: info@gullybaba.com
info@degreewala.com
WebSite: www.gullybaba.com,
www.ignouonline.com

2010 Edition

Author : Dinesh Verma, A.K.Saini
Price : 230/-
ISBN: 978-81-89086-39-8

Preface

This book is mainly targeted for BCA exam of Introduction to Foundation Course in English for Computing. It has been introduced in market after seeing the huge demand of ready to grasp material for exams with high level of quality, and its unavailability in market. We the GullyBaba Publishing House took a step ahead to publish the quality material focusing on exams at the same time giving you indepth knowledge about the subject.

GPH Book is the pioneer effort that provides a unique methodology so as to perform better in exams. If your goal is to attain higher grade use this powerful study tool independently or along with your text.

*On the Web : **www.gullybaba.com** is the vital resource for your exams acting as catalyst to boost up your preparation.*
*Now you can access us on the net through **www.doctorignou.com, www.doeacconline.com, www.gphindia.com, and www.gullybabapublishinghouse.com.***

Feedback about the book can be sent at **cs610writers@gullybaba.com.**

Acknowledgments :

We appreciate the staff and facility support provided by GullyBaba Publishing House. In particular, we appreciate the encouragement and professional advises received from Mr. S. Roy, Mr. Tarun Sharma, B. K. Krishna and many more.

Also we would like to thank typesetting and designing team Mrs. Bhawna Verma, Mr. Shravan Vats, Mr. Parveen Kumar, and Mr. Mukesh.

We gratefully acknowledges the significant contributions of Mr. Mahesh Chand, Mrs. Bimla Devi, Mrs. Bhawna Verma and our experts in bringing out this publication.

New Delhi **Publisher**

CONTENTS

STUDY MATERIAL

SOLVED PAPERS

Chapter - 1

Verb

Verb

Verb is a word that represents some action, feeling or existence. It basically tells us something about the subject; for example :

> Girls **fly** kites (Action)
> Hello, I **feel** sorry (Feeling)
> Smt. Indira Gandhi **was** the Prime Minister of India (existence)

The number and person of their subjects limit the verbs shown above in black. Therefore, fly, feel and 'was' are Main Verbs. Main verbs are also called as Finite Verbs and was is also an Auxiliary Verb.

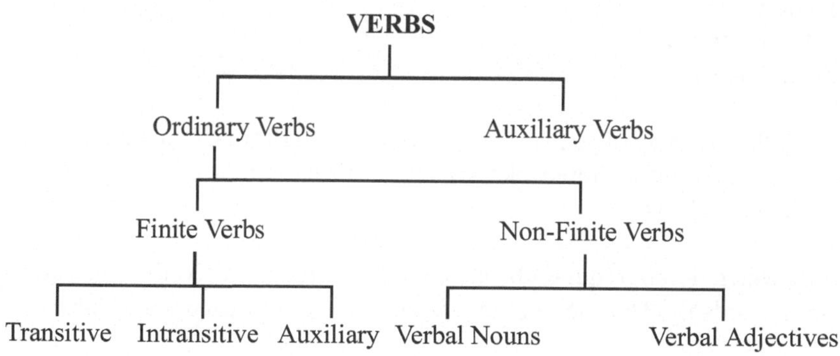

There are two types of verbs in English language :

1. Ordinary Verbs → Ordinary verbs are speak, tell, read, go, sit etc.
2. Auxiliary verbs → Auxiliary verbs are will, have, can, may, must, should, be, is am, are, was, were etc.

Ordinary Verbs are of two types :
(a) Finite verbs
(b) Non-finite verbs

Finite verbs are those who change their forms according to the person and number of subject and the tense also, for example :

I speak, He speaks and They spoke.
I go, she goes, they go

Non finite verbs are those who do not change their forms according to the number, person or tense of the subject. The infinitives, gerunds and participles are called non-finites verbs. They are classified into two types :

1. Verbal nouns e.g.
Infinitive : I want to go.
Gerund : Walking is a good exercise

2. Verbal adjectives e.g.
Present Participle : Flowing water is pure.
Past Participle : He gave me a broken inkpot.

Whereas finite verbs are classified into three types :
(i) Transitive
(ii) Intransitive and
(iii) Auxiliary

A verb that takes an object is called a Transitive verbs e.g. Sita Sang a song. I wrote a letter and Children like sweets. In these sentences song, letter and sweets are objects.

Verbs which do not require objects are called Intransitive Verbs e.g. The sun shines. Birds fly. The chair broke. Some verbs can be used both Transitively and Intransitively.

Verbs used intransitively	Verbs used Transitively
The table broke	She broke the glass
The horse runs fast	I ran a race
Woods float in water	He floated paper boats.

All the Transitive Verbs can be used intransitively in case they do not contain an object. Sohan is reading. Some transitive verbs require two objects called Direct and Indirect Objects. The verbs give, grant, ask, promise, offer, teach, tell, show, write etc. take two objects i.e. He gave me (Indirect Object) a gift (Direct Object). I gave him (Indirect Object) your message (Direct Object).

Some Intransitive Verbs are followed by a Noun which is similar in meaning to that of the Verb. They are called cognate object e.g.

I saw a wonderful sight
Let us run a race
He sang a melodious song.
He slept a sound sleep
They fought a brave fight

Verbs which do not make complete sense by themselves are called verbs of Incomplete Predication. To complete the sense, they require complements. They convey the idea of being, becoming and seeing; as :

(a) Intransitive Verbs of Incomplete Predication are : Be (is, am, are, was, were), seem, become, look, appear, grow, taste, turn, go etc.. For example :
They look happy
You appear to be sad
Man is mortal

(b) Transitive Verbs of Incomplete Predication are : Appoint, believe, call, create, elect, find, make, name, suppose, think, wish etc.. For example :

We called him a liar
They made him king
The judge found him guilty

The above verbs act as links between their subjects and the compliments. They are called Linking Verbs.

Verbs which denote a certain state or steady condition are called stative Linking Verbs. They are generally not used in the Present Progressive Tense. For example :

He seems restless
I remain unconvinced
Your argument sounds strange

There are certain other stative verbs besides these Linking Verbs; as :
See, hear, smell, feel, think, remember, want, like, love, have, own, contain etc. These verbs are also not used in the present progressive form. We will not say – I am seeing a child playing the garden. We should say – I see (or I can see) a child playing in the garden.

But the verbs which denote a process or a change in the person or thing mentioned in the subject are called the Dynamic Linking Verbs. They can be used in Present Progressive Tense as :

You are growing weaker and weaker
The milk is turning sour.

Transitive Verbs can be used Intransitively as follows :

(a) When no object is thought and the verb is used to express something in a general way. For example :

The truck stopped suddenly.
The girl cried all of a sudden.

(b) When the reflexive pronoun is omitted, as

I moved (myself) near the platform
Keep (yourself) to the right

The noun comes in the form of object (cognate object) with many Intransitive Verbs which has the meaning similar to the verb. They are used transitively as :

She died a natural death
Sohan sang a sweet song.

Here cognate object is used in the accusative case.

Some Intransitive Verbs are rendered into Transitive Verbs by adding some preposition with them e.g.

The police looked into the matter
Don't laugh at the poor beggar

It is seen that these prepositions are closely connected with the verbs. Their use in this way is called Prepositional Verbs.

When an Intransitive Verb is used in the causative sense and causes some action or thing to be done, it becomes a Transitive Verb. For example :

Intransitive	Transitive	
Ripe fruits fall on the ground	He felled the trees.	(caused to fall)
The horse runs	He ran the horse	(caused to run)

Subject Complement can be a noun or an adjective.

He is healthy	(Adjective)
He is a boy	(Noun)

✓ **Auxiliary Verbs** ⇒ It is a helping Verb, which helps a Principal or Main verb to form a tense, mood or voice; some question or negative sentence. For example :

1. He had (Auxiliary Verb) already reached (Principal Verb) home.
2. I play (Principal Verb) cricket
3. She has (Auxiliary Verb) finished (Principal Verb) her work
4. I shall (Auxiliary Verb) help (Principal Verb) you.

✓ **Chief Auxiliary Verbs** ⇒ are to be (is, am, are, was, were), to have (has, had), to do (does, did), may, might, can, could, shall, should, will, would, must etc.

Only Primary auxiliary Verbs can be used as finite or main verbs - These are be (is/am/are/was/were), do/does, have/has/had.

Do you smoke ?	(do – auxiliary verb)
I do my work	(do – main verb)
She has stolen my pencil	(has – auxiliary verb)
She has a new scooter	(has – main verb)

The Conjugation of Verbs – To conjugate a Verb means to give its four Principal forms: Present, Past, Past Participle, Present Participle.

If the Past or the Past Participle is formed from the Present Tense by changing the Vowel of a verb as take, took, taken and do, did, done; the Verb is said to be a Strong Verb.

If the Verbs require the addition of 'ed' 'd' or 't' to form their Past and Past Participles, they are called weak verbs as Died, died, died and built, built, build.

Present and Past Participle forms of certain verbs are alike for example

come, came, come,
run, ran, run

There are also finite verb and non finite or infinite verb. To understand the difference between them, look at these sentences :
1. He kills a snake
2. To kill a snake requires courage

In sentence 1, "he" is the subject of the verb kill. Therefore, it is controlled by the number and person of the subject. It cannot go beyond their domain. Therefore, it is a Finite Verb. Therefore, the Finite Verb is the verb which remains limited by its number and person and its meaning in present simple tense.

In sentence 2, to kill "To kill" expresses the action shown by "by" and in the absence of its subject it functions as the subject of the verb "requires". Thus its meaning in the form of an action is not governed by any subject, person or number. In other words its meaning is infinite. Hence it is termed as non-finite or infinite. Non-finites are of three types :

1. Infinitive
2. Gerund
3. Participle

1. Infinitive → It is the form of a verb which mentions in the abstract the action expressed by the Verb. Generally 'to' is placed before the Present form of the verb to form the Infinitives. For example to go, to come, to stand etc. But many verbs do not take 'to' (Infinitive) before them. The verbs which do not take 'to' before them are termed as 'bare Infinitives'
The Infinitive with 'to' is used as follows :

(a) After a Verb as an Adverb (called the infinitive of Purpose); as :
She stood to welcome me.
My mother went to the college to see the Principal

(b) After an Adjective as an Adverb; as :
Your father is angry to find you here.
I am delighted to see you here.

(c) After a Noun or Pronoun as an Adjective; as :
She has many books to read
I need water to drink

(d) After the verbs of knowing or understanding – know, feel, suppose, understand, consider, feel, think etc. as :
She knows how to drive the car
I consider him to be intelligent

Note : These Verbs used as main verbs can be followed by object + to be :
I consider him to be the best boy.
But it is much more common to use that + an ordinary tense :
I consider that he is the best boy.

(e) After adjective/adverb + enough
She is mature enough to understand it.
She is rich enough to lend you money.

(f) After too + adjective / adverb
It is too late to do anything now.
She is too young to understand.

Note : If the subject of both the sentences is common, they can be combined by using too + adjective / adverb + to (infinitive). But in case the subjects are different then take help from the second subject by putting the preposition 'for' before it and use the infinitive 'to' after it.

It is very hot. We cannot sit. = It is too hot for us to sit.

(g) After how / when / where / what + to infinitive
He did not know what to do.
I do not know how to swim.
Can you tell us where to find them ?
How can I say when to leave ?

(h) After it is / was + adjective + for / of you / him etc.
It is good of him to help you.
It was brave of her to catch the thief.
It is important for the students to understand the topic.

(i) To join two sentences in place of a clause
I went to the college. I met the Principal
= I went to the college to meet the Principal.

He went to the playground. He wanted to play.
= He went to the playground to play.

(j) The infinitive is used after only to express a disappointing sequel.
She went to the house only to find it burning.
She survived the crash only to die in the river.

(k) After the first, the second etc. the last, the only and sometimes after superlatives :
She was first to win a prize.
He was the best actor to act in this play.

The Infinitive is a Verbal Noun, used instead of a noun it performs all the functions of a Noun viz.

(a) As the subject of the verb :
To speak the truth is a virtue.
To drink is bad for your health.

Note : In case of a Dummy subject, 'It' is placed in place of 'to' Infinitive. In that case the Infinitive 'to' becomes the virtual subject.
It is a virtue to speak the truth.
It is bad for your health to drink.

(b) As the Object to a Verb :
They want to play.
I want to sleep now.

(c) As the Complement of a Verb:
His object is to marry this girl.
I want to be a teacher.

(d) As the Object of a Preposition :
She sat down to take rest.
They set out to search the boy.

(e) As an Object Complement :
I told her to distribute the sweets.
We helped them (to) engage a carpenter.

The Omission of 'to' – The 'to' of the Infinite is dropped after the verbs bid, dare, let, make, need, observe, fall, hear, see, watch, behold etc.. All the Verbs used after the Modal Verbs are infinitives without 'to' for example :

I let him go.
He can sit.
She made me run
I bade him go
I shall go.

You can sit.
You need not worry

But 'to' is not omitted when :
(i) The above mentioned verbs except, 'let' are used in the passive voice for example :
She was seen to ring the bell.
I was made to stand
The bucket was let fall into the well.

(ii) When 'dare' is used in the affirmative; as –
I dare to say this.
He dared to oppose his elder sister.

(a) But in the negative 'to' following need / dare (modal auxiliaries) is dropped.
I dare not go before him.
You need not go there.

But when need and dare are used in the form of main verbs, 'do' (auxiliary verb) and 'to' (infinitive) are not dropped.

Does Sohan need **to go** there ?
I do not need **to go** there as he himself is coming.
I do not dare **to go** bear feature.
Do you dare **to do** it ?

(b) After the auxiliary verbs;

You may **go** now.
She will **pass** this year
They do not **like** sweets.

(c) After 'but' and 'except'

You do nothing but **talk**.
I could not but **laugh**.
He does everything except **deceive** his friends.

(d) After had better, had rather, would rather etc. and 'than'

I would rather **starve** than **beg**.
He had rather **retire** than **work**.

2. Gerund → A gerund acts partly as a verb and partly as a Noun. It is formed by adding 'ing' to the first form of the verb. It is also called a **Verbal**

Noun. In form it is similar to the form of **Present Participle**. The only difference between a Gerund and a Present Participle is that a Gerund is used in the form of a Noun but the Present Participle is used as an Adjective.

3. Participle → A participle is a word which is partly a Verb and partly an Adjective. For example

I saw her writing a letter.

Here writing is a participle. It qualifies the object i.e. him; it is adjective as well as a verb.

There are three kinds of Participles.
They are :
(a) Present Participle
(b) Past Participle and
(c) Perfect Participle.

Chapter - 2

Adverbs

Adverbs are words which modify the meaning of a Verb, Adjective, a Preposition, a Conjunction or another Adverb. For example :

She is very honest.	(very–Adverb qualifying adjective honest)
He struck me exactly on the head.	(exactly – Adverb qualifying the preposition on)
This horse runs fast.	(fast – Adverb qualifying verb runs)
I solve the question simply because it was easy.	(simply Adverb qualifying another adverb because)

Sometimes an Adverb modifies the entire sentence. For example :

Unfortunately he lost his mother.
(This type of Adverb is called an Adjunct in Grammar)
Probably he is mistaken.

There are three kinds of Adverbs :

1. Simple Adverbs
2. Interrogative Adverbs
3. Relative Adverbs

1. Simple Adverbs → Simply modify some words. They are of following kinds :

(a) Adverbs of Time : Today, after, ago, then, before, tomorrow, formerly, recently, soon, shortly etc.
(b) Adverbs of Place : There, here, in, up, down, out, anywhere etc.
(c) Adverbs of Manner : Gladly, politely, well, ill, quickly etc.
(d) Adverbs of Degree or Quantity: Very, much, almost, more, quite, little, too, partly etc.
(e) Adverbs Affirmative or Negative : No, yes, not etc.
(f) Adverbs of Reasons : as, since, because etc.
(g) Adverbs of result : therefore, so, consequently.

(h) Adverbs of purpose : In order that, so that etc.
(i) Adverbs of concession or contrast : Although-yet, though-yet etc.

2. Interrogative Adverbs → They are used for asking questions. They show place, time, quantity, number, manner and cause e.g.

How are you now ?
Where does your mother live ? and
Why are you late ?

How, where, why, when, how far, how long etc. are **Interrogative Adverbs.**

3. Relative Adverbs → They join two clauses. It refers back to some antecedent; as :

Please tell me why you are late.
This is the house where I live.

✓ **Formation of Adverbs ⇒** Adverbs are formed :
(a) By Adding "ly" :
1. To nouns; as – yearly, weekly, hourly.
2. To Adjectives; as – kindly, wisely, slowly.
3. To Participles; as – hurriedly, lovingly.

(b) By adding Prepositions :
1. To nouns; as – afoot (a = on), ashore, abed, beside (be = by), to-day.
2. To Adjectives; as – aloud, behind, below, anew
3. To Participles; as – herein, hereby, henceforth.

(c) By Combining a Noun and an Adjective; as East-ward, side-ways, mid-day, some-times.

Chapter - 3

Conjunctions

Conjunction is a word used to join words, phrases, clauses and sentences. It also establishes a relation between the parts that have been joined. The major conjunctions used are : either, or, neither, nor, though, and, lest, unless, while, when, however, because, since, but, otherwise, therefore, yet, whether, if, both, till, as, like. It is divided into two classes :

1. Co-ordinate Conjunctions
2. Sub- ordinate Conjunctions

✓ **Co-ordinate Conjunctions** ⇒ Are those, which join words, clauses, phrases and sentence of equal rank or grammatical units of the same kind. For example :

> Go **and** bring me a chair.
> Give me tea **or** coffee.
> He is rich **but** not happy.

There are four types of co-ordinate conjunctions, in which co-ordinating clauses are joined.

✓ **(i) Cumulative Conjunctions** ⇒ They add one statement or a fact to another. These are :
As well as, both...and, too, now, also, not less than, not only ....but also. For example :

> She is not only rich but also clever.
> She is both intelligent and beautiful.
> Sohan is reading and his sister is writing.
> Mohan as well as his parents is illiterate.

✓ **(ii) Adversative Conjunctions** ⇒ They not only join two sentences but also show contrast between them. These are but, wherever, yet , still, nevertheless, however, only, while etc.. For example :

My uncle is rich, while my father is poor.
Sohan worked hard, nevertheless he failed.
Rahul felt angry but I kept quite.

✓ **(iii) Alternative Conjunctions** ⇒ They express a choice between two statements. These are : otherwise, or, else, either…or, neither ….. nor. For example :

Rahul has neither a car nor a scooter.
Work hard, otherwise you will fail.
Either you or Sohan is at fault.

✓ **(iv) Illative Conjunctions** ⇒ They show that one fact or statement is inferred, or proved from another. They, therefore, express inference. They are :

So, for, then, therefore

For example : He worked hard, therefore, he passed.
The bus is about to go, let us get in then.

3. Sub-ordinate Conjunctions → Sub-ordinate Conjunctions help to connect unequal functional value or subordinate clause or dependent clause to the Main Clause. Subordinate conjunctions are : so that, that, unless, if, until, in case, till, when, after, before, so long as, because, as long as, why, when, where, whether, as if, as soon as, as, than, while, since etc. For example :
He cannot come to school because he is ill.
I know that Sohan will come first in the class
Hardly had I reached the bus stand when it began to rain.

Subordinate Conjunctions are of nine kinds. They are :

✓ **(i) Time as** ⇒ when, before, as, as soon as, so long as, until, after, while since, as long as, till etc.. For example :
When she reached home, she was shivering with cold.
The patient had breathed his last before the doctor arrived.
Wait here till I come.
Do not move from this place until and unless I order.
Strike the iron while it is hot.
He has been staying with me since 1st October, 2004.
As he climbed higher, he got very tired.

✓ **(ii) Place; as** ⇒ wherever, where etc.. For example :
Go wherever you wish.
I know where you stay.

✓ **(iii) Cause or Reason; as** ⇒ since, because, as etc.. For example :
I cannot attend the meeting because I was busy with some other work.
Since(as) he is in trouble, I must help him.

✓ **(iv) Condition; as** ⇒ unless, only if, if, provided, whether etc.. For example :
You must go there whether you like it or not.
You can stay in my place provided you promise to leave no dirt.
Unless you work hard, you cannot pass.
I shall let you go only if (provided) you speak the truth.

✓ **(v) Purpose; as** ⇒ in order that, lest, so that, that etc. For example :
He ran fast lest he should miss the train.
She works hard so that she may pass.

✓ **(vi) Result or Effect; as** ⇒ such.....that, so.....that etc. For example :
You are such a rogue that nobody likes you.
He ran so fast that he was soon our of breath.

✓ **(vii) Comparison; as** ⇒ than, as much as, as .... As etc. For example :
She is as tall as her brother.
I can take as much as juice as you.
She is more beautiful than her sister.

✓ **(viii) Contrast or Concession; as** ⇒ notwithstanding that, however, though/although etc. For example :
Although/though he she worked hard, yet she failed.
You cannot pass, however, you may work hard.
They could not win, notwithstanding that they played well.

✓ **(ix) Manner or Extent; as** ⇒ as far as, so....as, if, as, according as etc. For example :
As far as I know, he is a very good worker.
He talks as if he was mad.
While in Pakistan, do as the Pakistani do.
The candidates were selected, as they were found fit.
Conjunctions serve as Sentence Connectors as well.

Chapter - 4

Article

A or **an** and **the** are known as Articles. They are really Demonstrative Adjectives. In other words, there are two Articles – a or an and the. A or an is called the Indefinite Article. It leaves the person or thing spoken of in an indefinite state; as

A file; that is, any file
An ox; that is, any ox.
Whereas The is called the Definite Article, which particularizes a person or thing e.g.

He ran after the thief. (some particular 'thief')

For better understanding the use of articles, it is essential to know something about nouns in English, since articles rightly belong to nouns. Most common nouns in English are either countable or uncountable. A countable noun is one that can be counted i.e. papers, books, holidays, cups etc.. These are called countable nouns. (How) many, a few and fewer can be used in front of them, whereas nouns which cannot be counted are known as uncountable nouns i.e. milk, rice etc., as we cannot say one milk, two rices, as in case of countable nouns.

An Article is commonly used before the Countable and Common Noun, Singular Number e.g.

> Here is a book for you.
> There comes an ox.
> This is the report I want.

When the Common Noun in Singular is used in a general sense, then no Article is used; e.g.

> Woman is vain.

Note : This statement is correct only in the case of a man and women.

Man cannot bear such humiliation (here man = all men)
But before other words, A means 'every one' : A cow has two horns means "Every cow has two horns"

Indefinite articles are used in the following ways :
(a) In numeral sense meaning one; for example :
Seven days are in a week.
I am a disco dancer.

(b) In the vague sense of something certain; for example :
In old days there was a kind in India.
One night a thief broke into her house.

(c) To represent a class; for example :
A student should obey his teacher.
A donkey is a beast of burden.

(d) To generalize the proper noun; for example :
He is a Newton. (as able as Newton)

(e) In the sense of the same; for example :
Birds of a feather flock together.

A is used with a word having a consonant sound whether the word begins with a vowel or a consonant; for example : a pen, a man, a book, a pencil, a unique building, a useful book, a European etc.

An is used before a word beginning with a vowel sound; e.g. an apple, an hour, an inkpot etc.
An is also used before words beginning with h and not accented on the first syllable; as An historical building, an hotel.

✓ **Use of the Definite Article 'The'** ⇒ 'The' is used to particularize a thing or a person, or one well-known to us or one already mentioned; e.g. Let us go to the market. I have lost the pencil that you gave me. The thief was taken to the police station. She sent me a book. The book was interesting.

When a Singular Noun represents the whole class; e.g. The lion is the king of beasts. The fox is a cunning animal.
The is also used when we wish to show similarity; e.g. Like Shakespeare, Kalidas is the first-rate poet in India. **The** can also be used with a Material

Noun when we change it into either 'of Phrase' or particularize it as a word or phrase or clause. The cotton of Egypt means especially cotton of Egypt. For example : The cotton of Egypt is superior to that of India. Gama was the Rustam of India. Always speak the truth.

With the names of oceans, gulfs, rivers, seas, groups of islands and mountain chain.

Before the names of sacred newspapers, magazines, well known buildings and sacred books.

Before the descriptive names of countries and provinces.

Before the names of unique objects

Before a Proper Noun when qualified by an Adjective or defining Adjective clause.

Chapter - 5

Prepositions

Preposition is a word placed before a Noun or a Pronoun to show its relation to some other word in the sentences e.g. She works hard in the hope of standing first. The loss of his son kept preying upon his mind. The Noun or Pronoun before which a preposition is placed is its object. It is in the Objective Case and is said to be governed by the proposition. For example : We waited for them. (not they). This pencil is for her (not she). She has no belief in me. (not I). Sometimes a Preposition follows the Object; as Here is a pencil that you were looking for. (The Relative Pronoun **that** is the Object). What are you driving at? (The Interrogative Pronoun **what** is the Object).

Prepositions are of five kinds :

1. Simple Prepositions → are after, at, by, down, in, over, of, up, to, with etc.

2. Compound Prepositions → are against, across, about, into, before, beside, until, within etc.

3. Double Prepositions → are from beneath, from under, out of, from among etc.

4. Participial Prepositions → are regarding, notwithstanding, accepting, considering etc.

5. Phrasal Prepositions → are on behalf of, in the event of, on account of, instead of, by virtue of, by way of, along with etc.

There are several dozens of prepositions, following are the prepositions commonly used :

1. At, In →

(a) At is used with the names of small villages and towns; whereas **In** is used with the names of big cities and countries; for example : She was born at Punjabi Bagh in Delhi. We settled at Delhi in India.

(i) At is used for a point of time.

(ii) In is used for a period of time.

For example : I shall see you at 8 O'clock in the morning.
I shall return in five days.

We say in the morning (evening or afternoon), at night, at dawn, at day break, at non etc..

2. After, In → When after and in denote time, the former refers to the pat and the latter to the future. For example : She came back after a year.
I shall return your book in a month.

3. After, behind → After refers to time, order or position whereas behind refers to place For example :

You came after 11 A.M. and stood behind the wall.
We ran after the thief.

4. Between, among → Between is used for two persons or things whereas among for more than two. For example :
The partnership between Ram and Shyam has been dissolved.
Distribute these bananas among all the girls.

5. In, Into → In shows rest within whereas into shows motion inwards. For example :
There are two almirah in the room
She jumped into the river.

6. In, within, before → In shows the end of a period of time; within shows the period before the end of a period of time and before refers to the time before a point of time. For example :
I shall write to you in a week. (during the week)
I shall write to you within a week (before the expiry of a week)
I shall finish this book before March, 2006.

7. On, Upon → There is no difference between on and upon. However, upon is more formal. For example:
The cups are lying on the table.
The king sat upon the throne.

8. Since, for, from → Since refers to a point of time, for to a period time. They are used in some forms of the Perfect Tense only. From is used for a point of time in any Tense. If since joins two clauses, we use Present Perfect before it (since) and simple past tense after it (since) however, we must keep in mind that since is not a preposition but a conjunction. For example :

I have been ill since Tuesday last.
It has been raining since morning.
We have not heard from you for a long time.
He has been working in this office for five years.
I shall wait for you from Monday to Friday.
He plays from morning till evening.

9. Besides, besides → Beside means by the side of whereas besides means in addition to. For example :

He was sitting beside his father.
Besides being punished, he was fined.

10. By, with → By refers to the doer or the agent whereas with shows the instrument. For example :

She was stabbed by her enemy with a dagger.
She beat me with a stick.
Also read the following sentences :

(a) He sat by his mother.	(It means that he sat near his mother)
I travelled by myself.	(It means that he travelled alone)
What is the time by your watch ?	(It means that what is the time according to your watch)
I am a Sharma by caste.	(It means that I am a Brahman in respect of caste)

(b) I rise with the sun.
With all your shortcomings, I like you.

11. Till, By → Till means upto whereas By means 'not later than'. By is also use for means of conveyance. For example :

I shall wait for you till 2 P.M.
I shall come back by 10 O' clock.
I went to Lucknow by Car.

12. Over, Above, Under, Below → Over is the opposite of under. Over implies the relation of highest in position or space. Above is the opposite of below and shows rest in a higher position. For example :

The roof is over the head.
My house is above the road.
She is under the thumb of her husband.
Her head is above water.
He is below me in the class.

13. Of → belonging to; form; about; having. For example :

The glass of this table is quite old.
He is a boy of much ability.
Nepal is in the north of India.

14. To → In the direction of, as far as, until, for the attention or possession of. For example :

He threw the ball to me.
She is busy from 2 o' clock to 5 o' clock
She sent a present to her husband.

Chapter - 6

Models

Read the Verbs in the sentences indicated in two columns below :

A	B
He himself did it	I have not written the lesson.
I have to go far	Did you learn your topic?
Mahatama Gandhi was a great leader.	The wounded were carried to the nearest hospital.
Man is mortal	It is raining.

It is seen from Column A above, the verbs is, was, have and did are used as full verbs. In column B they help the Principal Verbs (rain, carry, write, learn) to form Tenses, Interrogative or Negative sentences. They are called Helping or Auxiliary Verbs. They help to form certain grammatical constructions.

Helping/Auxiliary Verbs are helpful in forming Tenses, Questions (Interrogative sentences), Negative sentences and Passive Voice. Therefore, auxiliary verbs are those verbs which help other verbs to form their tense, mood ad shade of meaning etc.

Be, have and do are Primary Auxiliaries. Their forms are :

Be – be, am, are, is, were, was, being, been
Have – have, having, had, has
Do – do, done, doing, did, does

The Primary Auxiliaries (Be, have and do) change their form according to the number and person of the Subject; as I have, but, I do, he has, but, I am, he does, he is, but, he was, they were, they were, but. They are used to help in the formation of tenses, questions, interrogative, negative and voices whenever they are used in combination with main verb. They can also be used alone. Then they function as the main verb.

Shall, should, will, would, can, could, may, might, must, ought, used to, need and dare are modal auxiliaries.

Model Auxiliaries do not change (their form) according to the gender and number of the subject; as

You can, he can, I can, they can, she can,

Modal Auxiliaries are called Modals because they express the mode or manner of the actions denoted by the main verbs – whether the work can be done or not; whether the action should take place or not; whether the action is necessary or not; whether there is hope for the completion of the work or not.

Primary Auxiliary changes its form according to the number and person of the subject, whereas modal auxiliary remains unchanged. For example :

Primary Auxiliary : He has washed the shirts.
They have washed the shirts
He is washing the shirts
We are washing the shirts.

Modal Auxiliary : He can dance.
I can dance
They can dance
She can dance.

Modal Auxiliary is not used alone but is always used with the main verb whereas Primary Auxiliary can be used alone and in the form of the main verb too. For example :

You should not abuse him.
They must obey you.

I have a car.
He is a solider in the army.

Before we discuss their important uses, it is necessary to remember the following rules about the form of models :

1. They do not take the final 's' or 'es' in the third person singular : she can, he may, it must.
2. As in the case of other auxiliaries, they come before the word not in negative clauses and before the subject in interrogative sentences : She will not/won't come today or what can he do.
3. The past forms like could, might, should, would must do not express specially past tense : They should see their doctor here, should be used for future time.
4. In perfect and continuous tenses, they are not used because they don't have infinitive or partially form. An infinitive here is used without to after them : You must read. He may come.
5. Since they don't have infinitive and participate form, they cannot be used

in all tenses and do not change according to the number and person of the subject.

❖ USES OF THE MODAL AUXILIARIES

Use of Shall :

(a) Shall is used to express the future when subject is I or We. When shall is used with I and We, it does not denote the speaker's desire. As it means that 'I shall probably do so' or 'I may (be constrained) to do so'. For example :
I shall be twenty one next month.
I do not know whether I shall be able to join you.
If we walk fast, we shall catch the bus.

(b) Shall is used to express command, threat, compulsion, promise, certainty etc. for the second and third persons. For example :
If you win the match, you shall have a holiday. = Promise
If you run fast, you shall catch the bus. = Certainty
You shall be fined if you do not pay your renewal fee in time. = Threat
He shall carry out my orders = Compulsion

(c) In a statement shall is used to express the will, determination or intention; not of the subject, but of the speaker. For example :
She is my daughter. She shall have the best education.
So long as you are with me, you shall never feel short of money.
Here you shall have mangoes for the picking.

(d) When shall is used as shall I, it has two meanings :
1. to seek advice (counsel) from each other
My car is old, Sohan, shall I sell it?
2. When we are ready/willing to do some service to somebody and ask the will or desire of the person addressed. For example :
Ramu, you look to be tired, shall I work for you for some time?
3. Shall be also means proposal. For example : Shall we play hockey?
✓ **Will ⇒** Will with the second and the third persons denotes simple future tense but it expresses promise, determination, intention, wish, probability or likelihood, refusal, request invitation with the first person as :
I will pay your money tomorrow. (promise)
I will never tell a lie. (Determination)
I will punish you, if you do not speak the truth. (Threat)
We will help him (wish)
I will go to Lucknow. (Intention)

You will have heard the news (Probability or likelihood)
Will you carry this bag for me? (Request)
You will go to Delhi. (Order).

Shall or will used in Interrogative sentences shows intention or wish of the speaker e.g.

Shall I help you?
Will you play a match?
Shall he visit your house?
Shall we go for a picnic on Monday?
Will you please show me your computer?

✓ **Should** ⇒ Should is the past tense of shall. Should is used to express :
(a) sensible action or obligation, duty, advise e.g.
You should take bath daily.
He should speak the reality.

(b) In the Indirect Speech to express the Past Tense; e.g.
She asked me if I should help her.
He told me that he should reach home at night.

(c) logical necessity or probability, influence/deduction; e.g.
My pant should be ready by now.
He should be with his ailing mother at this time.

(d) probable condition: e.g.
Should he dishonest to you, report it to me.
Should she come here, give her my message.

(e) a report for permission; e.g.
I should like to inform that it was Sohan who broke the window pane.
I should like to inform you that I am not at fault.

(f) unexpected-ness or surprise; e.g.
That she should top the list.
It is really sad that he should lose his only daughter.

Should is also used as :
If she were here, I should like to see her. (Unreal condition)
Should you pass your examination, I shall give you a prize. (Condition)

You should not buy this house in ruin condition. (Suggestion)
You should not keep later hours. (Advice)
Work hard otherwise you should fail. (Purpose)
He should have spoken the truth. (but he didn't) (Past)

Should + perfect infinitive (have + verb in III form) expresses the sensible action. In case it occurs in the negative, it would mean that the action which has been done was not essential.

You should not have plucked the flowers. (but you did and it was not required)
You should have met him in the office today.

The word 'lest' is always followed by should but not with negative word.
✓ **Would** ⇒ It is the Past Tense of 'will'. It is used to express :
(i) the Past Tense of will or shall in the Indirect speech; as
He said that he would also fly kites.
They said that they would carry the day.
Direct : You said, "I shall take the test tomorrow."
Indirect : You said that you would take the test the next day.

(ii) a past habit; as

Now and then a black bird would call.
After lunch she would go out for a walk.
In winter she would study till late at night.

(iii) a preference or wish; as

I would rather have a cup of tea than milk.
He would rather break than stoop.

(iv) a wish or desire; as

I would like to explain my ideas.
Would (that) he were here at this time.

(v) a suggestion or polite request; as

Would you please show me your bag?
Would you please give me a glass of water?

(vi) the unreal condition or imagined result; as

I you had invited me, I would have come.
Had you helped him, he would have passed.

(vii) determination or intention; as

I would never leave you in the lurch.

I would have my say.

(viii) a not very hopeful wish relating to the future :

I wish it would stop raining.

(ix) Feel sorry in the matter that someone is unwilling to do something which the speaker either approves of or disapproves; as

I wish he would go to college. (I am sorry he does not go to College)

I wish she would not keep talking about herself. (I am sorry she keeps talking about herself)

If only plus would expresses regret about an action which is the alternative for if only plus past tense. In that case its meaning will be the same as that of wish/would.

✓ **Use of Can ⇒** It means 'be able to' or 'know how to'. It is used to :

(i) Express ability, temporary or permanent; as

I can beat him.

He can speak English fluently.

(ii) Express possibility; as

Anything can happen to him on the way.

Any good student can solve this problem.

(iii) Grant permission; as

Can I go home now, Sir ?

You can show me your homework in the afternoon.

For getting permission, 'May' shows more politeness and courtesy that 'can'.

(iv) 'Can't help' means 'can't avoid'. It is used in an idiomatic sense; as

She is a woman. She can't help weeping.

It is so funny. I can't help laughing.

✓ **Use of Could ⇒** It is the Past Tense of 'Can'. It is used to :

(i) Express the Past Tense of 'can' in the Reported Speech; as

He said that I could also sing.

She asked me if I could help him.

(ii) Express ability; as

He could not win the match.

I could solve all the problems.

(iii) Express a polite request; as

Could you show me your book ?

Could I consult you in this matter again ?

(iv) Express negative deduction; as

She says that she is still reading a novel.
She couldn't be still reading it.

Could plus perfect infinitive (i.e. could plus have plus verb in III form) is used for past ability when the :

(i) Action was not performed : He could have stopped the bus (but he didn't)

(ii) We don't know whether it was performed or not : The money has disappeared.

Who could have taken it ?

✓ **Use of Ought ⇒** Ought is followed by the Infinitive with 'to'. It is used to express duty, and a moral or social binding. The duty and moral or social binding is something internal. The speaker only reminds the listener about it. It is effective.

We ought to respect our seniors.
You ought to perform your duties.
He ought to serve his old mother.
You ought to have obeyed your Principal.

Perfect infinitive plus ought to denotes the incomplete duty or sensible action, which was neglected. Nevertheless, if the sentence is in negative it means that the action which has been completed should not have been performed; as
You ought not to have met her.

Use of May, Might

'May' is used to seek permission, express possibility or probably purpose, wish or prayer; as

May I go, Sir ?	(Permission)
It may rain today.	(Possibility, probability)
We eat so that we may live.	(Purpose)
May God bless you.	(wish or prayer)

When the main verb is in the past tense, we cannot use may : might must be used.

He told me that she might come.

'Might' is the past tense of 'may'. It is used to express :

The Past Tense of 'May' in the Reported Speech; as

I said that he might take my car.
He asked me if he might come in.

A doubtful possibility; as

She might come by the night flight.
The inspector might inspect the building.

(iii) It is also used in persuasive requests. It shows the speaker's anger because some action has not been completed; as

You might tell his father what he said, means please tell his father or I am annoyed that you did not tell his father what he said.

(iv) 'You might' can also express the casual command wherein the speaker has the certainty that his command will be obeyed.

You might post this letter, means kindly post this letter for me, will you?

✓ **Use of Must** ⇒ It is used to express :

(i) Obligation, necessity or emphatic advice, compulsion; as

We must respect our elders. (Obligation)
She must be admitted to the hospital. (Necessity)
He must attend the class regularly. (Emphatic advice)
He must work hard. (Compulsion)

(ii) Determination; as

I must get pass marks.
He must be around sixty.

(iii) Possibility or inference; as

He must have reached home by now.
There must be a mistake somewhere in writing.
She must be around sixty.

(iv) Logical necessity; as

It is raining. You must take your umbrella with you.
Who came into the classroom? That must be the peon.
You must take exercise to keep the body healthy.

(v) Must plus perfect infinitive (must plus have plus verb in III form) shows inference at present about some past action. Must not plus perfect infinitive shows that action which has been done was not needed.

He killed a lion. He must have been very brave.
He must not have gone there (there was no necessity of it)

The contracted form of 'must not' is 'Mustn't'. It represents negative obligation in present or future. Life 'Must', 'Must not' too shows the authority or strong advice of the speaker.

✓ **Use of 'Used to'** ⇒ It expresses a habit in the Past. It has no Present Tense form. It is always used in the Past; as

I used to go out for shopping. (but now I don't)
I used to drink daily. (now I don't)
He used not to play truant in school. (Negative, now he does)

Used he to smoke ? (Interrogative)

Used to also means 'to be habituated.' In such sentences 'used to' is preceded by be/seem/get/become etc.; as

I am not used to work in the Sun.

Please, behave yourself, I am not used to this kind of malafide intention.

✓ **Use of 'Need'** ⇒ As a **Principal Verb**, 'need' means 'to stand in need of'. Its three forms are need, needed and needed.

He needs money (Present)

I needed your help in studies. (Past)

She needs to consult you (Present)

He will need my help. (Future)

She does not need your help. (Negative)

As a **Defective Verb**, 'need' implies the absence of necessity or obligation. It is used in the Present Tense. It takes an infinitive without 'to' as its object; as

You need not work now. (absence of necessity)

You need not to bother about me.

He need not to wait for me.

You needn't give him a lift. He has his own car.

✓ **Use of Dare** ⇒ **(i)** As a Principal Verb, 'dare' means 'to challenge' or 'disobey' defy orders'. It admits of the forms dare (dares), dared, dared. It is used in all tenses and requires 'to' to complete it; as

I dare to say that you are a liar.

He dared to risk his life

She dares to go into the dark.

(ii) As a Defective Verb, 'dare' means 'to take courage or to venture.' It admits of forms dare, durst (dared), durst (dared). It is used (only) in the negative and interrogative sentences. 'To' is not required to complete it; as

He dare not say so. (Present)

She durst not opposite me. (Past)

How dare you enter the gate ? (Present)

How durst he abuse you ? (Past)

Chapter - 7

Reporting Speech

There are two different ways of reporting the words of a speaker :
1. Direct Speech
2. Indirect Speech

1. Direct Speech → It contains the actual words of the speaker; as
Mohan said, "My brother has a roaring business in Chandigarh."
The actual words of the speaker are indicated in the inverted comas without any change.

2. Indirect Speech → It gives the substance of the speaker's actual words and not the exact words spoken by him or her; as
Mohan said that his brother had a roaring business in Chandigarh.
The actual words of the speaker, indicated within inverted commas are called the Reporting Speech. The verb which introduces the Reporting Speech is called the Reporting Verb.

Some distinctive points regarding the Direct Speed and Indirect Speech are indicated below :

(a) In the Direct Speech :
(i) The Reported Speech is put within inverted commas.
(ii) A comma separates the Reported Speech and the Reporting Verb.
(iii)The first word of the Reported Speech begins with a capital letter.
(iv) In the Reported Speech we may use any Tense required by the sense and any kind of sentence.

(b) In the Indirect Speech :
(i) The inverted commas are removed.
(ii) The comma separating the Reporting Verb from the Reporting Speech is removed.
(iii)Reported Speech is introduced by some conjunction i.e. that, what, why, if etc.
(iv) Reporting Verb changes according to the sense.

(v) The Tense of the Reporting Verb is never changed.
(vi) All kind of sentences change into Assertive ones.

There are certain rules for the transformation of Direct Speech into Indirect Speech. These are :

1. The Tense of the Verb in the Reported Speech does not change, if the Reporting Verb is in the Present or Future Tense e.g.
✓ **Direct** ⇒ Mohan says, "Rita has brought a fair name to her family"
✓ **Indirect** ⇒ Mohan says that Rita has brought a fair name to her family.

✓ **Direct** ⇒ I shall say, "I went to Mathura on Tuesday."
✓ **Indirect** ⇒ I shall say that I went to Mathura on Tuesday.

2. If the Reporting Verb is in the Past Tense, the verb in the Reported Speech must be changed into the corresponding Past Tense e.g.
✓ **Direct** ⇒ I said, "I am speaking the lie."
✓ **Indirect** ⇒ I said that I was speaking the lie.

✓ **Direct** ⇒ We said, "They cannot cross the river unless the boatmen help them."
✓ **Indirect** ⇒ We said that they could not cross the river unless the boatmen helped them.

When it is necessary to change the tense of a verb, the following types of changes are usually made:

Direct Speech	Indirect Speech
He is	he was
He can	he could
He is reading	he was reading
He may	he might
He teaches	he taught
He was teaching	he had been teaching
He has taught	he had taught
He taught	he had taught
He will teach	he would teach
He will have taught	he would have taught]
He was taught	he had been taught

Demonstrative adjectives and adverbs of time and place usually change to denote a passage of time and a change of place :

Direct Speech	Indirect Speech
This	that
These	those
Now	then
Yesterday	the day before or the previous day
Last night/week/month/year	the night before/the week before/ the previous week etc.
Today/tonight	that day/that night
Tomorrow	the day after/the following day/the next day
Next week/month/year	the week after/the following week etc.
Here	there
Just	then
Day before yesterday	the day before the previous day
Day after tomorrow	the day after the next day

Change of Verbs :

1.	Is or am	changes into	was
	Are	changes into	were
	Has or have	changes into	had
2.	Present Indefinite	changes into	Past Indefinite
	Tell or tells (1st form)	changes into	told (2nd form)
	Do or does	changes into	did
3.	Present continuous	changes into	Past Continuous
	Is, am or are telling	changes into	was or were telling.
4.	Present Perfect	changes into	Past Perfect
	Has or have told		had told
5.	Present Perfect	changes into	Past Perfect
	continuous	changes into	continuous
	Has or have been Telling.	changes into	had been telling
6.	Past Indefinite	changes into	Past Perfect
	Told (did tell)	changes into	had told
7.	Past Continuous	changes into	Past Perfect Continuous
	Was or were telling	changes into	had been telling.
8.	Will	changes into	would
	Shall	changes to	should/would
9.	May	changes to	might
	Can	changes to	could

Must/	changes to	must
Had to	changes	had to

Exceptions :

1. If there is Universal Truth or Habitual fact in the Reporting Speech, the Tense of the verb is never changed; as

(i) Direct :- She said, 'Face is the index of mind." (Proverbial truth)

Indirect :- She said that face is the index of mind.

(ii) Direct :- The teacher said, "The earth rotates around its axis." (Geographical truth)

Indirect :- The teacher said that the earth rotates around it axis.

(iii) Direct :- His uncle, : "Two and two make four and not five:" (Factual truth)

Indirect :- His uncle said that two and two make four and not five.

2. The Tense of the Verb in the Reported Speech does not change if the reported speech states a past historical fact; as

(i) Direct :– She said, "India became free on 15th August, 1947.

Indirect :– She said that India became free on 15 th August, 1947.

(ii)Direct :– He said, "Her father lived at Lahore for ten years."

Indirect – He said that her father lived at Lahore for ten years.

3. If two such actions are given in the Reported Speech which take place at the same time, the Past Indefinite or continuous Tent is not changed e.g.

Direct :- He said, "Mohan was signing a song while Gopal was playing on a flute.

Indirect :- He said that Mohan was signing a song while Gopal was playing on a flute.

4. If the Reported Speech contains some Improbable or Hypothetical (imaginary) condition, Past Indefinite Tense does not change; as

Direct :- He said to me that, "If I were there, I would snub him.

Indirect :- He told me that if we were there, he would snub him.

✓ **From Indirect Speech to Direct Speech** ⇒ Following rules are to be followed:

1. Change Verb in the Past Tense in Indirect Speech into the corresponding Present Tense in the Direct Form according to the sense.
2. Put Direct Speech within Inverted Commas ("…………..").

3. Separate the Reported Speech from the Reporting Verb by a Comma.
4. Change the Reporting Verb into a suitable form of 'say'.
5. Change the Pronouns according to the sense.
6. Change words showing remoteness and distance by the corresponding words showing nearness.

For example :
Indirect :- I told her that she had not returned my pen even that day.
Direct :- I said to her, "You have not returned my pen even today."
Indirect :- She said that her uncle sent her a nice dress.
Direct :- She said, "My uncle has sent me a nice dress."
Indirect :- She told him that he had never lent her any book.
Direct :- She said to him, "You have never lent me any book."

✓ **Imperative Sentences** ⇒ Points to be remembered :
Change the Reporting Verb according to the sense as :
1. Request : request, beg, ask, entreat, appeal, etc.
2. Advice : exhort, urge, advise, forbid etc.
3. Order : command, tell, order etc.
4. The Imperative word is changed into Infinitive one.
5. No Conjunction is used to introduce the Reported Speech.
6. If the Conjunction 'that' is used, 'should' is placed before the infinitive.
7. Observe the rules for the change of Pronouns and words showing nearness.
8. Change the pronouns and words showing remoteness as per rules.

An Imperative Sentence is the sentence which expresses some request, advice, order or invitation; as

"Prepare a cup of milk for me" (Order)
"Don't smoke" (Advice)
"Have a cup of tea with us, please" (invitation)

One of the specialties of an Imperative Sentence is that it begins with a Verb. It has no subject. The reason behind the absence of the subject is that its subject is the person you are talking to. In other words 'You' is always its subject. It is discourteous to say 'you' in English.
While changing an Imperative sentence from Direct to Indirect Speech :
We change the Reporting Verb – said into ordered. But we do this only when some big officer or authority gives an order; as

The Chairman said – The Chairman ordered.

But when the elderly people ask the younger ones to do something we change said into told; as

Mother said to me – Mother told me.

But when the younger ones say something to the elderly ones we change said into asked; as

I said my mother – I asked mother

Then we remove Comma or inverted Commas (, "………") and connect the reported speech with 'to' (infinitive with to); as

Indirect :- Father said to mother. "Go and wash your hands."

Direct :- Father told me to go and wash my hands.

If a request has been made, we chane said into requested or begged and connect the reported speech with to.

Direct :- The beggar said to me, "Give me a rupee for a cup of tea, please."

Indirect :- The beggar begged of me a rupee for a cup of tea.

'Beg' is followed by 'of' in case of a person and by 'for' in case of a thing.

In case there is an invitation, said is changed into invited and in case of advice it is changed into advised.

In case the sentence is negative, we connect the reporting speech with not to. For example :

Direct :- Teacher said to the boys, "Don't make a noise."

Indirect :- Teacher ordered the boys not to make a noise.

In case there is some mode of address in reported speech as – my son, my daughter etc. used by the speaker for his own son or daughter, make it the object of the reporting verb; as

Direct :- The old man said to his child "My son, don't make a noise."

Indirect :- The old man told his son not to make a noise.

In case somebody addresses someone as my son or my daughter out of affection we shall connect it in the following manner :

Direct :- The beggar said to Sita, "My daughter, give me a rupee for a cup of tea."

Indirect :- Calling Sita his daughter, the beggar begged of her a rupee for a cup of tea.

✓ **Indirect to Direct Speech** ⇒ Change the Reporting Verbs – requested, advised, invited, told, ordered etc. into 'said'.

If the reporting verb has an object, put a comma after the object. In case there is no object, put the Comma after the reporting verb. Then put inverted commas or commas. Then change the pronoun of the reported speech and remove 'to'; as

Indirect :– The General ordered the soldiers to attack the enemy and destroy their defenses.
Direct :- The General said, "Soldiers, attack the enemy and destroy their defenses."

Indirect :- The thief requested the Magistrate respectfully to pardon him and then promised to lead a better life.
Direct :- The thief said to the Magistrate, "Sir, pardon me please, I promise to lead a better life."

Exclamatory Sentences

Conversion of Exclamatory Sentences from Direct Speech to Indirect Speech: Chane the Reporting Verb into exclaim, cry, applaud, confess etc. Also use – 'with joy', 'with wonder', 'with surprise', 'with disgust' etc. according to the sense of the sentence; e.g. exclaimed with wonder, cried with joy.

Change the Exclamatory Sentences into Assertive ones and replace sign of exclamation (!) with a Full Stop(.). Began the Reporting Speech with 'That'

Replace the expressions of Interjections and Exclamations with suitable Adverbs or Adverse Phrases according to the sense.

For example :
Direct :- He said, "Alas! We were ruined."
Indirect :- He exclaimed sorrowfully that they were ruined.
Direct :- He said, "What a great tragedy!."
Indirect :- He exclaimed in surprise that it was a very great tragedy.

Direct :- He said to the Officer, "May you live long!"
Indirect :- He prayed that the officer might live long.

Indirect to Direct :
Indirect :- The king angrily called them cowards and ordered them to be off.
Direct :- The king said, "Cowards! Be off."
Indirect :- The chairman exclaimed in surprise that she had made a big mistake.
Direct :- The chairman said to her, "Ah me ! you have made a big mistake."

Chapter - 8

Active And Passive Voice

Read and note the difference between the following two sentences :

Sohan sings a song

A song is sung by Sohan.

It is seen that practically there is no difference in the meanings of these two sentences. There are two different ways of interpreting the same thing. But in the first sentence the Subject performs the action while in the second sentence, the Subject of the Verb is acted upon. It means that it (the Subject) becomes the object of the Verb of the first sentence. Thus the voice shows whether the Subject of a Verb acts or is acted upon.

✓ **Interrogative Sentences** ⇒ Following are the rules to be remembered before converting the Interrogative Sentences from Direct to Indirect Speech:

1. The Reporting Verb is changed, into 'ask, enquire, inquire or demand' etc.
2. No conjunction is used to introduce the Reported Speech if the question begins with (an interrogative) word; such as who, what, which, whose, when, where, why, how etc.
3. If or whether is used to introduce the Reported Speech if the question is in Yes/No and begins with a helping verb – is, am, are, was, were, has, have, had, do, does, did, shall, will, can, could, should, would, may, might, must etc.
4. If the sense of 'must', 'necessity' or 'compulsion' is shown at the time of speaking, it will be changed into 'had to'. If the same 'necessity' or 'compulsion' shows the future, it will be changed into 'would have to'. It would remain unchanged if it shows 'permanent ruling' or 'prohibition'.
5. Change the questions into statements. Put full stop in place of mark of interrogation (?)
6. Observe the rules while you change Tense of the Verb, pronouns and words showing nearness.

'That' never introduces the Reporting Speech in the Interrogative Sentences. Enquire, inquire and demand take 'of' before a Personal Object.

For example :
Direct :- Ram said to Shyam, "Are you not my brother?"
Indirect :- Ram asked Shyam if he was not his brother.

Direct :- He said to me, "Will you take part in games?"
Indirect :- He asked me if I would take part in games.

Direct :- I said to her, "Will you have ironed your clothes?"
Indirect :- I asked her if she would have ironed her clothes.

Direct :- I said to him, "Do you want to go to Patna?" He said, "No, sir".
Indirect :- I asked him if he wanted to go to Patna and he replied in negative.

Direct :- I said to him, "Why did you travel first class."
Indirect :- I asked him why he had traveled first class.

Direct :- He said to them, "Whose book had you stolen".
Indirect :- He asked them whose book they had stolen.

✓ **From Indirect into Direct ⇒** Following rules are to be followed :
1. Change the Tense in Indirect Speech into its Corresponding tense form according to the sense.
2. Put Direct Speech into inverted Commas ("..................")
3. Put a Comma between the Reporting Verb and the Reported Speech.
4. Use 'said' in place of asked / enquired of / demand of etc.
5. Put the Interrogative words at the beginning of the Reporting Speech.
6. Put the Interrogative sign at the end of the Reporting Speech after you have changed it into statements.
7. Change the pronouns and words showing nearness according to the rule.

For Example :
Indirect :- He asked us if she slept.
Direct :- He said to us, "Does she sleep?"

Indirect :- I inquired of my sister which book she had bought the day before.
Direct :- I said to my sister, "Which book did you buy yesterday".

Indirect :- The teacher asked the boys, if he wanted him to revise the lesson again.
Direct :- The teacher said to the boys, "Do you want me to revise the lesson again."

When the subject of a Verb acts, the Verb is said to be in **Active Voice**; as

Lata sings a song.
I made a mistake.

When the object of the Active Voice becomes the subject, the Verb is said to be in the **Passive Voice**; as

A song is sung by Lata.
A mistake was made by me.

The Subject dominates in Active Voice but the Object dominates in Passive Voice.
(It is only the form of verb in a sentence which shows whether the subject is the doer or the receiver of the action)

Following to be followed while changing a verb from the Active Voice into the Passive Voice :
1. If the object group (because sometimes a group of three – four words can also be an object) of the Active Verb is made the subject of the passive verb.
2. If the Subject of the Active Verb is made the object of some Preposition (generally 'by')
3. The Verb of the Active Voice must have the Past Participle form of the Finite Verb and some form of the verb 'to be' (be, am, is, are, will be, has been, is being etc.) will be used before it.
4. The Passive Verb must have the Past Participle form of the Finite Verb.
5. Some form of the Verb 'to be' is used according to the sense.
6. Some vague and indefinite subjects like 'everyone', 'they', 'people', 'someone', 'somebody', 'everybody', 'anybody' etc. are dropped when they are thought to be changed into subjects.
7. Some vague and uncertain subjects like 'they', 'everyone', 'someone', 'people', 'everybody', 'somebody', 'anybody', etc. are omitted when it is accepted that they are understood to have been changed in the Subject.
8. The Tense of the Verb does not change.

For Example : She has done his work. (Active)
Her work has been done by him. (Passive)

The Pronouns (when these act as subject) are changed as under :

Subject		**Object**
I	becomes	me
We	becomes	us
You	becomes	you
She	becomes	her
He	becomes	him
They	becomes	them

It	becomes	it
Who	becomes	whom

In the following sentences the Intransitive Verbs have no Objects. They cannot be changed into the Passive Voice :

The birds fly in the air.
These horses run fast.

Only transitive verbs can be changed into passive voice and not the intransitive verbs.

Present Indefinite or Simple Present Tense :

(i) Affirmative Sentences → In passive voice is/am/are + verb in third form is used; as

Active	Passive
He likes me.	I am liked by him.
We teach you.	You are taught by us.

(ii) Negative Sentences → As indicated above in affirmative sentences, but 'not' is added to is/am/are and the helping verb do/does is dropped.

Active	Passive
He does not likes me.	I am not liked by him.
We do not teach you.	You are not taught by us.

(iii) Interrogative Sentences → While changing these sentences into Passive Voice, put is/am/are before the subject and past participle after it. The helping verb – do/does are never used in passive voice.

Active	Passive
Does he like me?	Am I liked by him ?
Do we teach you?	Are you taught by us?

(iv) Negative Interrogative Sentences → While changing these sentences into passive voice, put 'is/am/are' before the subject and put 'not' before the past participle.

Active	Passive
Does he not like me?	Am I not liked by him ?
Do we not teach you?	Are you not taught by us?

Present Continuous Tense :

(i) Affirmative Sentences → In passive voice is/am/are + being are added to the past participle form of the verb; as

Active	Passive
You are liking me.	I am being liked by you.
We are teaching you.	You are being taught by us.

(ii) Negative Sentences → 'Is/am/are+not+being+third' form of the verb i.e. past participle.

Active	Passive
You are not liking me.	I am not being liked by you.
We are not teaching you.	You are not being taught by us.

(iii) Interrogative Sentences → 'Is/are/am' is placed before the subject and 'being+past participle' after the subject.

Active	Passive
Are you liking me?	Am I being liked by you ?
Are we teaching you?	Are you being taught by us?

(iv) Negative Interrogative Sentences → While changing these sentences into passive voice, put 'is/am/are' before the subject and 'not+being+ past participle, after the subject.

Active	Passive
Are you not liking me?	Am I not being liked by you ?
Are we not teaching you?	Are you not being taught by us?

Present Perfect Tense :

(i) Affirmative Sentences → In passive voice has/have+been+verb in third form is used.

Active	Passive
He has liking me.	I have been liked by him.
We have taught you.	You have been taught by us.

(ii) Negative Sentences → 'has/have+not+been+ past participle form of the verb is used.

Active	Passive
He has not liked me.	I have not been liked by him.
We have not taught you.	You have not been taught by us.

(iii) Interrogative Sentences → Add has/have before the subject and 'been+past participle' after the subject.

Active	Passive
Has he liked me?	Have I been liked by him ?
Have we taught you?	Have you been taught by us?

(iv) Negative Interrogative Sentences → As indicated in the interrogative sentences above but 'not' is added before 'been' .

Active	Passive
Has he not liked me?	Have I not been liked by him ?
Have we not taught you?	Have you not been taught by us?

Past Indefinite or Simple Past Tense :

(i) Affirmative Sentences → In passive voice was/were+verb in third form is used.

Active	Passive
He liked me.	I was liked by him.
We taught you.	You were taught by us.

(ii) Negative Sentences → Negative sentences are changed into passive voice in the similar way as in Affirmative sentences. The only difference is that 'did' is removed and 'was not' or 'were not' are used before past participle in passive voice.

Active	Passive
He did not like me.	I was not liked by him.
We did not teach you.	You were not taught by us.

(iii) Interrogative Sentences → They are also same as Interrogative Sentences above. 'Did' is removed and 'was/were' is put before the subject.

Active	Passive
Did he like me?	Was I liked by him ?
Did we teach you?	Were you taught by us?

(iv) Negative Interrogative Sentences → It is also same as Interrogative Sentences given above. The 'not' added with the verb of the Active Voice and is placed before the past participle in passive voice.

Active	Passive
Did he not like me?	Was I not liked by him ?
Did we not teach you?	Were you not taught by us?

Past Continuous Tense :

(i) Affirmative Sentences → To change into passive voice, 'was/were+being+past participle' is used.

Active	Passive
He was liking me.	I was being liked by him.
We were teaching you.	You were being taught by us.

(ii) Negative Sentences → To change into passive voice, 'was/were+not+being+past participle' is used.

Active	Passive
He was not liking me.	I was not being liked by him.
We were not teaching you.	You were not being taught by us.

(iii) Interrogative Sentences → By adding 'was/were' before the subject of the passive voice and putting 'being+past participle after the subject.

Active	Passive
Was he liking me?	Was I being liked by him ?
Were we teaching you?	Were you being taught by us?

(iv) Negative Interrogative Sentences → By adding 'was/were' before the subject of the passive voice and putting not + being + past participle after the subject.

Active	Passive
Was he not liking me?	Was I not being liked by him ?
Were we not teaching you?	Were you not being taught by us?

Past Perfect Tense :

(i) Affirmative Sentences → To change into passive voice, 'had+been+past participle' is used.

Active	Passive
He had liked me.	I had been liked by him.
We had taught you.	You had been taught by us.

(ii) Negative Sentences → To change into passive voice, 'had+not+been+past participle' is used.

Active	Passive
He had not liked me.	I had not been liked by him.
We had not taught you.	You had not been taught by us.

(iii) Interrogative Sentences → By adding 'had' before the subject and 'been+past participle after the subject.

Active	Passive
Had he liked me?	Had I been liked by him ?
Had we taught you?	Had you been taught by us?

(iv) Negative Interrogative Sentences → By adding 'had' before the passive subject and 'not + been + past participle after the subject.

Active	Passive
Had he not liked me?	Had I not been liked by him ?
Had we not taught you?	Had you not been taught by us?

Future Indefinite Tense :

(i) Affirmative Sentences → To change into passive voice, 'shall/will+be+past participle' is used.

Active	Passive
He will like me.	I shall be liked by him.
We shall teach you.	You shall be taught by us.

(ii) Negative Sentences → To change into passive voice, 'shall/will+not+past participle' is used.

Active	Passive
He will not like me.	I shall not be liked by him.
We shall not teach you.	You will not be taught by us.

(iii) Interrogative Sentences → To change them into passive voice, place 'shall/will' before the subject and 'be+past participle after it.

Active	Passive
Will he like me?	Shall I be liked by him ?
Shall we teach you?	Will you be taught by us?

(iv) Negative Interrogative Sentences → Place 'shall/will' before the subject and 'not+be or +not+past participle after it.

Active	Passive
Will he not like me?	Shall I not be liked by him ?
Shall we not teach you?	Will you not be taught by us?

Future Perfect Tense :

(i) Affirmative Sentences → To change into passive voice, 'will/shall/will+have+3rd form of the verb is used.

Active	Passive
He will have liked me.	I shall have been liked by him.
We shall have taught you.	You will have been taught by us.

(ii) Negative Sentences → To change into passive voice, 'will/shall+not+have+been+past participle' is used.

Active	Passive
He will not have liked me.	I shall not have been liked by him.
We shall not have taught you.	You will not have been taught by us.

(iii) Interrogative Sentences → To change them into passive voice, 'shall/ will' before the subject and 'have+been+past participle after it.

Active	Passive
Will he have liked me?	Shall I have been liked by him ?
Shall we have taught you?	Will you have been taught by us?

(iv) Negative Interrogative Sentences → Place 'shall/will' before the subject and 'have+not+been+past participle after it.

Active	Passive
Will he not have liked me?	Shall I have not been liked by him?
Shall we not have taught you?	Will you not be taught by us?

Chapter - 9

Paragraph Writing

A paragraph is a group of sentences, which explain one single Thought or Theme. These sentences are interconnected in such as way that the Paragraph gives out one tone or tenor which is connected to its title. A paragraph has small ideas or thoughts, which add to the Main Thought.

It must be noted that an Essay comprises of many paragraphs. So, they should not misunderstand a paragraph as an essay and should not add irrelevant ideas to it.

Salient Features of a Paragraph :

1. Unity → It is the chief quality. All sentences must have unity and qualify a single thought or idea.

2. Order → It is the natural flow of small ideas or thoughts which look in sequence and natural in relation to the main thought.

3. Length → A paragraph should not be unusually lengthy.

4. Variety → The sentences in a paragraph should be both small and long, so that it looks beautiful and well-formed.

How to Write a Paragraph :

A paragraph expresses only one thought or idea. Hints given to a paragraph in the examination are wide. To write a paragraph based on them:

(i) Read all those hints again and again, so that the subject becomes clearer.
(ii) Keep the unity of the paragraph in mind.
(iii) Start writing the paragraph in a proper sequence.
(iv) Frame sentences from those hints. First and the last sentences should confirm the Theme.
(v) Express only one Thought or Idea in one paragraph.

Solved Papers
CS-610

CS-610 FOUNDATION COURSE IN ENGLISH FOR COMPUTING
JUNE 2000

Note: *Answer all questions.*

Q1. Read the passage given below and then answer the questions which are based on what is stated or implied in the passage:

It seems distance has ceased to bother mankind. You can exchange letters and your thoughts with someone, despite thousands of miles separating you, in a matter of few seconds. If you so desire. The wonders of today's communications, or means of it, have taken enormous proportions, not to mention those of information technology. Whoever said that the world is shrinking day by day couldn't have been more true. As the twilight years of the last century came to an end, it became a more confirmed assertion.

Communication is making *that* happen. As always, necessity is the cornerstone of all new discoveries and inventions. The latest in the electronic media being the much talked about and advocated INTERNET. If you've heard the word, its only natural. Special features on Internet dailies, magazines and the overall media have made it virtually impossible to get off the mark upheld as a phenomenon. Internet is being referred to as the ultimate in electronic democracy.

All you need to tap this marvellous reservoir of information sounds incredible - a telephone line, a modem computer and an Internet connection. And what can you do? Well, exchange letters and thoughts is just the tip of the iceberg. Much more ! You can scan scientific articles, see advertisements at your will, do shopping, select tourist spots in Australia with ideal boarding and lodging places, information on travel guides sitting here in India, enjoy jokes, movies, in this no holds barred means of communication. Time is not far when Internet access will be available through cable network.

(i) Why does distance not bother mankind today? [2]

(ii) What does the word 'that' refer to in paragraph 2? [2]

(iii) What two things would you like to do with Internet? [2]

(iv) Give another word similar in meaning to: [2]

(a) wonders

(b) enormous

as given in the passage.

(v) Give a word opposite in meaning to: [2]

(a) incredible

(b) shrinking

(i) Distance does not bother mankind today, because we can exchange letters and our thoughts with anyone thousands of miles away, in a matter of few seconds due to advancement in the information technology.

(ii) The word 'that' refers to in paragraph 2 communicate the wonders of today's communication.

(iii)The two things I would like to do with Internet are :

(a) Sending/receiving messages through e-mail

(b) Chatting.

(iv)wonders - miracle

enormous - immense

(v) incredible - credible

shrinking - expanding

Q2. Fill in the blanks with the correct form of the verb given in brackets:

(a) She____________ (go) abroad every year. **[6]**

(b) He ____________ (drink) coffee every morning.

(c) He ____________ (work) for an hour.

(d) He ____________ (return) before I left the shop.

(e) The quality of the onions ___________ (be) not good.

(f) Either Mohan or Ram ____________ (have) stolen the watch.

(a) goes

(b) drinks

(c) has been working

(d) had returned

(e) is

(f) had

Q3. Do as directed: **[8]**

(a) ____________ girl in red dress is my daughter.

(insert an article)

(b) He is ________________ honourable man.

(insert an article)

(c) The work was done __________ haste.

(insert a preposition)

(d) She said, "We were thinking of selling the house but we have decided not to."

(change into reported speech)

(e) "You'd better not drink the water till it has been boiled," she said.

(change into reported speech)

(f) If I lived near the office ________________.

(complete the sentence)

(g) He is very weak, He cannot walk,
(combine the two sentences into one simple sentence)
(h) I bought a book yesterday. It has been stolen.
(combine the two sentences into one complex sentence)

(a) The
(b) an
(c) in
(d) She told that they had been thinking of selling the house but had decided not to.
(e) She told me not to drink water till it had been boiled.
(f) I would have come before
(g) He is too weak to walk.
(h) I bought a book yesterday which has been stolen.

Q4. Rewrite the following in passive voice: **[6]**
(a) I remember my father taking me to the circus.
(b) They threw away all the old magazines.
(c) Who broke this vase?
(d) I have warned you of the danger.
(e) He made us work.
(f) She will keep her jewellery in the safe

(a) My father taking me to circus is remembered by me.
(b) All the old magazines were thrown away by them.
(c) By whom was that vase broken?
(d) You have been warned by me of the danger.
(e) We were made to work by him.
(f) Her jewellery will be kept in the safe by her.

Q5. Write a paragraph not exceeding 150 words on any *one* of the following topics: **[8]**
(i) Importance of Discipline in Life
(ii) The Telephone
(iii) Fast Food Culture
(iv) Leisure

✓ **(i) Importance of Discipline in Life ⇒** Discipline is the law of nature and plays a very vital role in human life. Hence, there is a necessity to follow and observe discipline in all respect. It is the back bone of a country/organisation. A country/organisation can not progress until discipline is observed through out the country/organisation in all sphere of various departments. Defence is an ideal example of discipline. In defence forces, if there is no discipline, the country will go logs. Even Mahatma Gandhi has said that it is not the duty of a soldier to criticise the orders of his officer. His duty is only to obey. If we evaluate a person's personal life, we see that a person who is well disciplined, his life will be quite happy, if he is not following his time table of daily routine, his life will be miserable. As can be seen, nature is also following the law. The sun rises in the morning and sets in the evening regularly. The seasons come and go in proper order annually. Day and night alternate each other. It means that heavenly bodies all observe discipline. Let us try to develop 'discipline' in us. That can be started from childhood. A disciplined person is not only an asset to himself but also to his family/society/nation and mankind as a whole.

✓ **(ii) The Telephone** ⇒ The telephone is a means of quick communication. It was invented by Graham Bell in a period of long time. Now, it has become a part of necessity in human life. In ancient times, people were using drums to draw the attention of the people living far away and sending letters through pigeons. Today in case we have to talk to our friends, relatives, who are living hundreds/thousands of kilometers away from our place of living can be contacted on dialing his/her numbers and within a span of time we start talking. In a few second, we can exchange feelings, views, thoughts on phone and listen his voice as if he is looking to us. Telephone is the cheapest source of communication. Now a days, due to advancement of technology in telephone industry, telephones are being used as answering machines, fax and even for Internet. It can also be seen that telephone is not only a source of communication, but also used for transfer of data, pictures, music etc. through Internet by telephone cables by connecting telephone connection with computers. The latest generation of telephone is mobile telephones. If you have the mobile telephone number of a person having mobile phone, you can talk to him without any hindrance even if he is in the bathroom.

✓ **(iii) Fast Food Culture** ⇒ Fast food is any food that is quick, cheap, and convenient. Fast food culture is the generation of western countries in India. It is now being followed and liked by Indians too. At present Pizza, Burger, Chowmin are the most popular fast foods. Now a days, number of outlets in the name and style of McDonald's, Nirula's, Pizza Hut have been opened at Railway Stations, Inter State Bus Terminals and at the prime locations for serving variety of fast foods. They are the best known places for having a taste of variety of fast foods. The reasons of attraction of people towards fast food are : People has developed their food habits and taste in other culture food and it is easily and quickly available in the markets. The fast food is becoming so popular that it has become a type of fashion, students, elders and children are also becoming a prey of this culture. They are very fond of eating fast food. No one has time to ponder over its effect. It's true that fast food is usually high in fat, calories, cholesterol, and sodium, but eating fast food every once in a while is not going to cause you problems. If you eat too much fast food over a long period of time, though, it can lead to health problems like obesity, high blood pressure, and heart disease. But in any way it is not befitting the taste of our country.

✓ **(iv) Leisure** ⇒ The actual meaning of leisure is time available for ease and relaxation. Now a days, man is working like a machine. He is always seen busy in doing this or that work. Sometimes he has no time to look after of his own health, his family or remember the Creator. If anybody does not have leisure time, his health will be down and automatically his efficiency of working will decrease. It is well expressed that work while you work and play while you play. Man will definitely loose his capacity of work if he does not take rest, entertain himself and keep himself from all tension of work. To provide more leisure to employees, the government is following five days a week, which means that Saturday and Sunday off. Even then government is providing leave travel concession to their employees once in two years for home town and once in four years to any where in India. In this direction the Western countries are more forward. They are providing free visit to any country to get fresh and to bring back their energies. For those who are earning more can have a choice of working off the strains of the day at InShape – the Fitness Centre with its modern gymnasium, sauna, steam & whirlpool facilities. They can also avail the facility of rejuvenating body massages, in both ancient Indian and International styles. Leisure can be enjoyed by following one or the other hobby. We can read some enchanting books. We can follow the hobby of stamp collecting or gardening or photography or we can see some religious movie or domestic TV serial. The best way of passing a happy life is that one should divide both work and leisure in such a way that neither leisure hampers work nor work put obstacle upon the leisure. Both goes on side by side without hindering each other.

Q6. Write a composition in about 350-400 words on any *one* of the following topics: [12]

(a) The Advantages of Distance Learning

(b) Science in the Service of Mankind

(c) Books: An Investment

(d) Environmental Pollution

✓ **(a) The Advantages of Distance Learning** ⇒ Distance Learning is an emerging industry that utilises technology to provide and administer higher education and corporate training. Its rapid growth is propelled by the space sector, Internet and the enormous opportunity embedded in global education.

The main advantage of distance learning is that it allows students to study at a time, pace and place convenient to their needs. Learning can therefore be integrated into existing commitments whether they be professional, personal or domestic. Because of this, distance learning is an increasingly popular method of course delivery for busy professionals wishing to update their practice or continue their academic development. Students can also benefit from the trend within the University towards mixed mode delivery where students can choose a certain component of their course to be undertaken by distance learning. For the working class, many universities have started such courses long back, such type of learning is called distance learning. Assignments are sent by post, one can attempt them and send back for evaluation and correction. Tests and examinations are held regularly and promotion is gathered for next higher standard. Degree is also awarded. This type of study does not affect your service and a lot of time and money is saved. These universities have opened their study centers in all the major cities where the classes are conducted mainly on holidays. Important information is being provided at the centers. A very good knowledge is imparted by these institutions. The admission criteria of these universities is transparent and very simple. An over age person get an opportunity to enhance his skills by taking admission. Students have the option to study anywhere they like and study at their own sweet will. Students are also given sufficient time to finish their courses. For a graduate level course, the student can finish his programme between 3 to 8 years and can be registered again after 8 years if he likes to continue. Another advantage is that a very large number of students can be enrolled by a single university. The overall cost factor for the study including classes being organised at different institutions is also less, as compared with that of a full time course from a regular university. The study materials are delivered by registered post at the doorstep of the students. The Distance Learning India 2003 international conference provided an integrative model to enhance the learning environment through technology and provide a framework for redesigning instructional processes to achieve highly efficient and effective learning environments that supersede the geographic distance barrier.

The approaching reality of distance learning experiences, computer-centric school education, instant and enterprise-wide corporate training, and so on has made distance learning a crucial topic. The interest surrounding distance learning is created by the space / satellite segment, and the Internet's ability to rapidly deliver vast amounts of educational content.

The one-day international conference with the theme "Distance Learning - The New Frontiers" has created a forum for the distance learning sector to upgrade the expertise, technology and services to concerned users, authorities and corporate organisations.

✓ **(b) Science in the Service of Mankind ⇒** Science has contributed us with a number of marvellous things, out of which some are amazing. Science has provided us with new and useful things in all sector of human life i.e. transportation, communication, medical science, agriculture, information technology, internet, computer, entertainment and so on. All these achievements of science have not come to man as a ripe apple falls from a tree in the lap of a man sitting underneath. Science is not only the result of observation and experience but is the result of centuries of hard work done by him without bothering about his life. For example Madam Curie sufferred from cancer while experimenting with x-rays emitted by radioactive radium. Burno was burnt alive. Science has proved a blessing to the mankind. People are spending a luxurious life. Right from the morning till night whatever we see, we use, we think, is all science and nothing else. We should be grateful to our forefathers who thought and worked so hard for us to bring out countless scientific devices and appliances for comfort.

Brand new areas of scientific discovery have emerged in recent years with the development of new technologies. If you compare the past with the present, the difference seems as a dream. What more to say, the man has reached the moon and is further trying to go on their planets. The discovery of electricity is the achievements of twentieth century. The electricity contributes in its string innumerable devices like fluorescent tube, bulb, fan, desert cooler, air-conditioner, geyser, heater, electric iron, electric oven, washing machine, mixer etc.. Also the printing presses, textile mills, factories, computers, TV sets etc. are also functioning with the help of electricity. Today, we need not to wait for electricity in case of power failure, we have generators and inverters which save our time. Now we have fast cars, trains, buses, trucks, trains, aeroplanes, ships and so on.

The most significant achievements of science are in the field of medicine and surgery. Now drugs are available for incurable diseases. All tests of operations are very easy. The old people whose eye sight was diminishing can see with the help of simple operation, the most painful diseases are under the control of the doctor. Also the crops good seeds and fertilizers have increased the food production. The another blessing of science is invention of telephone. Now one can talk to one's near relatives and friends in any corner of the world. It seems that the distance has converged and we can exchange our ideas within a second or so. The another very useful and excellent invention is Internet. Through Internet we can exchange our ideas within a second from one end to the other end of the world. But, despite these progresses, an enormous number of needs continue to remain .

✓ **(c) Books : An Investment ⇒** Books : An Investment, is true but even then they are the source of knowledge and the real friend of man. The value of books does not change, even after the invention of so many new things by the science. The books carry all the soundness of the past ages, as they are often compose by immensely learned and experienced men and women. To respect the books means to respect our past. As we need food to serve our body, similarly books serve the purpose of food to our mind. The company of books is far better than that of friends because we are always guided by the books, in our life whereas a friend can misguide. Therefore, purchasing of books is timely investment. Books are very precious for us because they enhance our knowledge. We have not seen our ancestors, but with the help of book we learn about the lives of our ancestors. We learn how they were successful in some fields and why they failed in others. A great statesman of the past impart their sound advise to us through medium of books.

There are different types of books are available in the market, but the most beneficial books are those which force us to think.

There are numbers of books which have universal truth; for example Vedas, Granthas, Upanishadas, Purans, Ramayan, Mahabharat, Geeta, Bhagawat etc.. These books were written by the ancient times learned saints. Their theme and concept remains unaltered even today. These books not only give immense pleasure but also compel us to investigate our birth in this world.

In today's world, a large number of professions are there to study, so as to study these professions a large number of books have been developed and are available in the market. There are books on literature and science, languages, arts, on sports, music, health, education, technology, space, mountaining, astrology, chess, defence, astronomy, reikhi, feng sui, acupuncture, horticulture, cooking, starring, cartooning, painting, drawing, embossing, computers, commerce, business, marketing, management, yoga, meditation, engineering etc. They are our genuine guide. They always show us the true path, when we follow the same we can make our birth truthful. We can also represent them as immortal. They not only make us fresh but also provide a practical direction.

✓ **(d) Environmental Pollution ⇒ In the present scenario, the major cause of pollutions are from air, water, food and noise.** The most essential need of human body to survive is fresh air, clean water and good food. Now a days the entire environment is polluted. Some places are polluted due to long chain of traffic standing for a considerably long period due to traffic jam, while the others due to increase in number of vehicles plying on roads. Also there is a considerable increase in number of factories and mills emitting polluted air constantly. The other cause of pollution is cutting of green fields and experimentation of atoms and war in Iraq. There is no fresh air to breathe and pure water to drink. The cutting of green fields has adversely affected the rain fall. The air pollution is mainly caused due to emission of Carbon dioxide, lead oxide not only by the vehicles but also from the generators being used in industries and households. Some industries and factories, themselves give up the pollutants and circulate them into the atmospheric air from where they are inhaled by animals, plants and human beings. The polluted environment has given birth to a number of illnesses like asthma, Tuberculosis, Lung cancer, skin problem, irritation in eyes etc.. The pollution levels are on the increase day by day in all the industrial and urban areas of India.

For living a heathy life, everybody should have to be more careful in this direction. Also the government should take remedial and corrective action to save our natural phenomenon. They should have to take concrete steps to stop the pollution. At present, the government has taken a very appreciable step that is introduction of CNG buses instead of diesel. All buses have been converted into CNG from diesel. This has reduced the pollution level to some extent. Though the scientists are of the opinion that they have got victory over the nature but it is not true. Nature keeps the balance of its bionomics in many ways like floods, earth quakes, draught etc.. The second type of pollution is water pollution. Water pollution is mainly caused from the waste being thrown by industries and households, which have resulted in water pollution of the rivers. Due to essential need of a human being and frequent consumption of polluted water, many people suffer from various diseases like dysentery, dehydration, viral fever etc.. The next type of pollution is that of food. Due to frequent use of dangerous fertilizers and pesticides, the food has become polluted. Lastly, the noise pollution is caused from industrial noise, noise of vehicles plying and noise of human. This pollution has added problems like hypertension, blood pressure and mental instability in the life of human beings. We must seek some concrete solutions for these problems that we are knowingly facing. Government has taken a serious note of these and has introduced CNG buses for reducing the pollution. Pollution can only be reduced if every one pay attention towards it and protect the natural gifts provided by the God, otherwise in the coming years, it will become very difficult to survive in such an unhealthy environment.

CS-610 : FOUNDATION COURSE IN ENGLISH FOR COMPUTING
JAN 2001

Note: *Answer all the questions.*

Q1. Read the passage given below and answer the questions which are based on it.

To achieve the full potential of computers in education requires that educators, programmers and computer manufacturers will need to evaluate the computer based materials for the schools. The evaluation of a computer system must integrate a variety of evaluation techniques to assess the computer program effectively. Educators need to use the computer program skilfully. The major consideration in evaluation should be the degree to which the product fits the particular uses for which it is considered.

Second-language teaching through computers is an area where such evaluation is very useful. Second-language teaching presents the challenge for creating and locating courseware which encourages students to think creatively about language.

One of the main advantages of using a computer-assisted instructional system is the ease with which the second-language can be assessed and intervention materials be used a common graphics base.

(i) Say whether the following statements are true or false: [5]

(a) Computers have no place in second-language teaching

(b) Educators need to use the computer program skilfully.

(c) Second-language teaching presents no challenges.

(d) Students need to think creatively about language.

(e) An important consideration is whether the product fits the particular use for which it is considered.

(a) False

(b) True

(c) False

(d) True

(e) True

(ii) Should the evaluation of a computer system follow a single evaluation technique or should it integrate a variety of them? [3]

The evaluation of a computer system should integrate a variety of evaluation techniques to effectively assess the computer programmes.

(iii) What kind of challenge does second-language teaching present?[3]

Second language teaching presents the challenge for creating and locating courseware which encourages students to think creatively about the language.

(iv) What are three categories of professions that will need to evaluate computer based materials for schools? [3]

The three categories of professions that will need to evaluate computer based materials for schools are :

(a) Educators

(b) Programmers

(c) Computer manufacturers.

Q2. Fill in the blanks with the correct form of the verb given in the brackets : [6]

(a) Recently air fares have___________(go) down.

(b) Gopal___________(go) to a gymnasium every morning.

(c) He________(die) as soon as the car hit him.

(d) It_________(rain) since last night.

(e) He________(ring) me up last week.

(f) The fire________(be) brought under control with difficulty.

(a) gone

(b) goes

(c) died

(d) has been raining

(e) rang

(f) was

Q3. Do as directed? [5]

(a) It has been raining for__________hour. (Insert an article)

(b) He said to me, "How old is your father? "

(Change into reported speech)

(c) He has applied_________two posts. (Insert a preposition)

(d) If__________ I shall give you that book.

(Complete the sentence)

(e) This college has________excellent playground.

(Insert an article)

(a) an

(b) He asked me how old my father was ?

(c) He has applied for two posts.

(d) available

(e) an

Q4. Rewrite the following in passive voice : [5]

(a) Have you read that book?
(b) He will never hurt me.
(c) He stole a scooter.
(d) Can you lift this bag?
(e) The teacher greeted the children.

(a) Has that book been read by you ?
(b) I shall never be hurt by him.
(c) A scooter was stolen by him.
(d) Can that bag be lifted by you ?
(e) The children were greeted by the teacher.

Q5. Write about 200 words on any *one* of the following : [10]

(a) Quiz Shows
(b) A Visit to a Book Fair
(c) Pollution in Delhi
(d) Your Favourite TV Serial

✓ **(a) Quiz Shows ⇒** At one time, quiz shows were being organised in the schools, colleges and sometimes in the clubs, but now a days quiz shows are often arranged on televisions. These quiz shows are very popular. By and large, quiz shows are arranged on T.V.s and questions are asked and after the competition is over the result is declared. The viewers of the TV take keen interest and also learn from these quiz shows. For taking participation in the quiz shows one has to learn and practice a lot. If it is quiz competition on science, then one has to have a thorough knowledge of all the science subjects. In general knowledge quiz show, one should have thorough knowledge of all the subjects, literature, social sciences,sports and games, ancient and current events, great personalities of the world politics and economics noble prize winners, great scientists way and treaties etc. It is not easy to take part and win such quiz shows. In short, quiz shows are very interesting and advantageous. Quiz shows are a very good source to enhance and check our knowledge. Quiz shows help students to practice their knowledge which enhances their confidence. The viewers get bulk knowledge regarding various things. Quiz shows are being organised on different topics. One of the topic is that of dowry system. One of the burring issue in India is dowry. These quiz programs may also help in changing the thinking of our older and younger generations. Regular quiz shows can be conducted to eliminate the social problems.

✓ **(b) A Visit to a Book Fair ⇒** There are number of fairs being organized in "Pragati Maidan", New Delhi. Out of these fairs, one is Book Fair, which is organised every year, where reputed publishers participate with their old and recent publications. In the book fair, all kind of books are available at reasonable prices. Sometimes those books, which are not available in the market, are also available in the fair. I am a regular visitor to Book fair for the last two years. Also the latest books on every subject are available in the book fair. This year also I went to the fair and the fair was very interesting and informatory. Books are true friends of man and in the fair we get a chance to get all the national and international books under a single roof. It is a kind of exhibition where books are decorated in the shops in a presentable way, so as to attract the visitors at a glance. Besides books for adult, children books are also available. Children can buy books of their choice. There are educational books on stories, comics, pictures etc. for children which they read and enhance their knowledge. This time I along with my parents visited the book fair at Pragati Maidan which was arranged in hall number ten. Most of the reputed Indian publishers participated in the fair and set up their stalls. I visited all the Indian as well as foreign stalls. I liked the foreign stalls more because of their aesthetic look. They had arranged all the books very systematically and in a presentable shape. I liked very much the Italian stall .They had brought the cheap editions of their best books for sale and also they are giving heavy discounts on them. I purchased almost a single copy of each book. They have also given me their literature book, as free gift, on the purchases made by me. It was really a great experience for me to buy books from a book fair under one roof. I also came across with various scholars, friends who had also come to see the fair and I enjoyed the fair a lot.

✓ **(c) Pollution in Delhi ⇒** In today's life in Delhi, pollution has became a part of life. Since morning till evening, people are facing the problem of pollution in one way or the other. It has become a great pain to the people in general. Public health is badly effected by the pollution. As you are aware, the pollution is of three kinds air pollution, water pollution and noise pollution. The main cause of pollution is due to increase in population. Due to increase in population, the cities are going to be crowdy day by day. The speedy urbanisation has pushed the urban residents to lead to a life full of pollution. At present, there is pollution and contamination in every ingredient which contribute to life, even in the medicines and hence pose a danger to the patients who seek physical relief from the same. The main cause of air pollution is due to increase in number of vehicles, plying and factories working which emits polluted air comprises of carbon oxide, carbon dioxide, nitrogen oxide, sulphar dioxide, oxides of lead etc. The inhalation of these substances leads to many diseases and respiratory problems. The increase in number of vehicles run on the roads, which give birth not only to polluted air but increases the noise pollution also. The polluted drinking water is also a problem everywhere. The water of yamuna river is also badly polluted. The dirty water from some of the factories and mills reaches to yamuna river through dirty nalas. These factories and mills were ordered by the Government to shift out of Delhi but the other political parties come in the way and the policy could not be materialised. With the conversion of buses from diesel to CNG, there has been a considerable improvement in the pollution level. Now all the buses have been made CNG compatible and their emissions does not have so much of pollution. Even some of the car owners have converted their cars from petrol to CNG gas. This conversion not only reduces the pollution level but also the cost of travel. The cost of petrol is much more than that of CNG gas. It is a good step taken by government to control the pollution level in Delhi.

✓ **(d) Your Favourite TV Serial ⇒** There are number of TV serials being broadcasted of T.V. and they were liked by people besides Doordarshan. Different type of serials are being aired by number of channels. Social serials relating to family matters are very much seen and liked by the people apart from the other serials, I like one of the entertainment serial 'Kaun Banega Karor Pati' hosted by Amitabh Bachhan on Star plus Channel. The time of the serial is from 09.00 PM to 10.00 P.M. and is aired from Friday to Sunday. This serial remains one of the most popular serial as compared with other serials. The entire credit of success to this serial goes to Amitabh Bachhan due to his style of presentation. His style of presentation is very enormous. A person who does not participate in the serial, still enjoys the same. In case the participant does not know the answer of a particular question, he is provided with three life line options for taking assistance to answer a question. The first one is from audience support, the second one is fifty fifty and the third one is phone a friend. The question asked for bears four options in which one is right and the remaining three are wrong answers. In case the player has any difficulty in answering or not sure of the answer, he utilises any or all the three life lines for getting the correct answer and he will be entitled for Rs.1000/- for the first correct answer, Rs.3000/- for second, Rs.5000/- for the third and double the amount in the proceeding correct answers. After reaching at the amount of Rs.20000/-, one help line with the name 'flip' is added and he will get Rs.20000/- in case of any wrong answer upto Rs.6,40,000/- and thereafter he will get Rs.6,40,000/- for any wrong answer upto Rs. Two Crores. In case anybody wants to quit the game, he is allowed to quit and get the winning amount. If he gives wrong answer to any question, then he gets the minimum slab amount fixed at the above mentioned levels. His entire winning amount will be deducted and he does not get anything, in case his answer is wrong upto Rs.10,000/-.

This serial always remains a source of education because it provides a lot of knowledge through questions being asked. I like this serial very much.

Q6. Write a dialogue of about 150 words between yourself and a friend on any one of the following: [10]

(a) Recent American Presidential Election

(b) Perils of noise

(c) Religious tolerance

(d) Should cricket be banned ?

(a) Recent American Presidential Election

Myself : Hello, Pawan, how are you and what are you reading in the newspaper. Do you know anything about recent Presidential Election going to be held in America.

Pawan : You have asked number of questions at a time. Any way, yes, I know about that Presidential Election going to be held in America. As Bill Clinton is going to be retired and also Bush has got more popularity in comparison to his opponent.

Myself : Yes, you are right, but I think Bush will become the President. Amongst Indians also his recent visit made him more popular.

Pawan : As you are aware, elections are conducted just to establish a healthy and social set up. Moreover, America is a democratic country and they believe in democracy which means for the public, of the public and by the public.

Myself : Yes, indeed Americans are very particular of their rights. Even the presidentials candidates come from the public to show their stand. They believe that they are not out of public.

Pawan : For the post of President, a right candidate who is lawful, honest, good person, great diplomat, good politician can be proved as a right candidate.

Myself : But, Mr. Bush's statement reveals that he would follow the same foreign policy as far as India is concerned. He said that he may prove better than Bush.

Pawan : But why Indian Government change its policy related to Americans.

Myself : I know, India has very good relations with Russia and it has helped a lot to India against America in the past. So, India is still inclines towards Russian.

Pawan : But there was a time when Russia and America were equivalent and these were known as two power blocks in the World. These two power blocks were headed each one block by them. These power blocks were maintaining balance in the world, now the situation has changed. So policies on foreign affairs should be changed.

Myself : It is right. Since Russia is not having the same equivalency to

America, still it is equally powerfull.

Pawan : Now the situation has changed. Americans are also trying to establish better relations with India. We have to think over it twice.

Myself : OK. I think that Bush has got better support and I am of the opinion that Bush will come as new President of America.

Pawan : Let us wait and watch the situation.

(b) Perils of noise

Myself : Hello, Pammi, how are you ? Do you know that perils of noise is on the increase ?

Pammi : I know, but there is no solution at present to overcome this problem.

Myself : The perils of noise are due to increase in vehicular traffic on the roads, noise of industries and the human but can you explain me what these problems are ?

Pammi : Blood pressure and mental instability in the urban masses are quite common due to noise. If the noise levels are not brought down, there are chances of depression, high blood pressure and other related psychological diseases would increase.

Myself : Pammi, is there anything being done to reduce the noise pollution ? Or any thing new has been introduced to check the noise pollution?

Pummi : To check the noise pollution emitted by loudspeakers, a device was invented.

Myself : Nothing can be done, unless there is a general awareness against noise pollution. People should show some interest.

Pammi : Also the noise pollution is more dangerous than an accident.

Myself : You are very right Pummi. Pollution is increasing continuously day by day.

Pummi : All types of pollutions can be tolerated except noise pollution. Noise pollution not only leads to mental torture but can also be a cause of deafness or even death.

Myself : I agree with you. Noise pollution is very dangerous.

Pummi : Have you seen that in a religious function at home, people are dancing on DJ with extremely high sound. They know that it can lead to deafness but they do not care.

Myself : Yes, some people do not bother about their neighbours who have to go to their offices or their children who have to appear in the examinations next morning. They continue dancing on DJ till late night. These type of things should be stopped.

(c) Religious tolerance

Myself : Hai, Pawan, do you know that religious tolerance means to extend religious freedom to people of all religions, even though you disagree with their beliefs and/or practices.

Pawan : Yes, I know. Also India is a secular country and there are old people who still blame something in the past for any mis-happenings. They are following their religion, beliefs and faiths without seeing.

Myself : But I do not understand why are these religious struggles, fighting, riots and enemity in the persons who follow different religious.

Pawan : This will continue as there is no peace among the nations without peace among the religions, no peace among religions without dialogue between the religions and finally no dialogue between the religions without investigation of the foundation of the religions.

Myself : I appreciate your suggestion but I am of the opinion that public in general is not concerned at all with such things. They should have that much religious clearance that they do not come in the way of other religions. There are number of Hindu and Muslim saints who have written about Ram and Krishna. Also some Muslims by caste and followers of Islam have got a honourable position in the history of Hindi literature. There are number of Hindi pandits who have written in Urdu and Farasi.

Pawan : That is all the religious tolerance. The best way is that everybody should follow good things of all the religious and should have equal regard to each and every religion.

(d) Should cricket be banned ?

Myself : Hello, Pawan, how are you and where were you ?

Pawan : Hello, I am fine and due to my illness, I was on leave and I have joined today only, how are you?

Myself : I am also fine. Do you know that cricket now a days is at its highest level of popularity and is at top of all games, not only in India but also in the world.

Pawan : Yes, it is the most popular game in the world.

Myself : Pawan, the recent happening of match fixing incidents have discouraged its popularity and have brought a bad name.

Pawan : I have heard about the match fixing scandals coming up in the news now a days. It is really a matter of shame. I was just surprised to listen this news.

Myself : You might be knowing that top most cricketers of the team are involved in this scandal and they are also found guilty.

Pawan : Now there is sufficient evidence available against them.

Myself : I do not know, inspite of getting more than enough money, not only from cricket, but from advertisement also , how can our cricketers do this.

Pawan : Now a days the cricketers want to generate more money, whether it is from advertisements, match or match-fixing. They have become greedy.

Myself : Some people are of the opinion that cricket should be banned.

Pawan : It should not be banned but the players found guilty of match fixing should be punished or debarred forever from playing cricket.

Myself : Your suggestion is good but I think it should be banned because it is a waste of time and money, people are mad after cricket. They do not do any work during the matches. A lot of money is wasted, after all what is the use of cricket.

Pawan : If you think so, then every thing should be banned, which is not useful. Basically, it is a source of entertainment.

CS-610 FOUNDATION COURSE IN ENGLISH FOR COMPUTING
JUNE 2001

Note : *Attempt all the questions.*

Q1. Read the passage given below and answer the questions which are based on it :

The technique of making the computer carry out a particular calculation is known as 'programming' which involves first breaking the calculation down into a sequence of arithmetic operations, and then preparing a series of instructions which cause the computer to carry out the required operations on the stored information in the correct order.

There are many situations in which the ability to handle and to analyse large quantities of arithmetic data according to instructions is of great value. Atomic physics and astronomy are some of the areas which come to mind. This ability also helps in the storage of reference data in libraries and other such places in such a way as to afford easy access to particular reference on request.

A particularly important application of the digital computer in simplified form is as a component in the control equipment of manufacturing processes.

(i) State whether the following statements are true or false : [5]

(a) Digital computers are of no use as a control equipment of manufacturing processes.

(b) The ability to handle large quantities of arithmetic data is useful in atomic physics.

(c) Libraries need to have easy access to particular references.

(d) A first step in 'programming' is breaking the calculation down to a sequence of arithmetic operations.

(e) Libraries are not meant to store reference data.

(a) False.

(b) True

(c) True

(d) True

(e) False

(ii) What are the two areas in which the ability to handle and to analyse large quantities of arithmetic data helps? [3]

The two areas in which the ability to handle and to analyse large quantities of arithmetic data helps are :

(1) Atomic physics (2) Astronomy

(iii) Does astronomy also benefit from the ability to handle and analyse large quantities of arithmetic data? [3]

Yes, astronomy also benefits from the ability to handle and analyse large quantities of arithmetic data.

(iv) What does 'programming' involve? [3]

Programming involves first breaking the calculation down into a sequence of arithmetic operations, and then preparing a series of instructions which cause the computer to carry out the required operations on the stored information in the correct order.

Q2. Fill in the blanks with the correct form of the verb given in the brackets: [6]

(a) Seeing _______________(be) believing.

(b) He __________________(fall) down from a tree last week.

(c) He has just ___________________ (finish) this novel.

(d) I have ___________________(know) him for many years.

(e) He was ___________________ (watch) TV when the earthquake came.

(f) Everyone of them ___________________ (know) the alphabet by heart.

(a) is

(b) fell

(c) finished

(d) known

(e) watching

(f) knows

Q3. Do as directed : [5]

(a) He bought ___________________umbrella last Monday.

(Insert an article)

(b) He has given ______________ smoking.

(Insert a preposition)

(c) He said to me, " Is the doctor at home?"

(Change into reported speech)

(d) I said to him, "Do you know Japanese?"

(Change into reported speech)

(e) Curfew has being lifted from some parts of the city. (Correct the sentence)

(a) an
(b) up
(c) He asked me if the doctor is at home ?
(d) I asked him if he knew Japanese ?
(e) Curfew has been lifted from some parts of the city.

Q4. Rewrite the following in passive voice : [5]
(a) Did he help you?
(b) Has he crossed the river?
(c) He is eating bananas.
(d) The police caught the thief.
(e) Mohan does not like Sohan.
(a) Was he helped by you ?
(b) Has the river been crossed by him ?
(c) Bananas are being eaten by him.
(d) The thief was caught by the police.
(e) Sohan is not liked by Mohan.

Q5. Write about 200 words on any *one* of the following : [10]
(a) Dishonesty in public life
(b) Traffic-jams
(c) The value of books
(d) A bad neighbour
✓ **(a) Dishonesty in public life** ⇒ In the ancient time people knows the value of each other. They believe and respect each other. They exchange things without any bad intention. They had the curiosity to help each other. But in the present scenario in India, dishonesty has become common in public life. Everybody seems to be running after money by all means whatever he likes. The picture of today is depressing and un-safe. To survive man has to struggle with these elements. In the competitive life to aline himself he turns dishonest. He only thinks of benefits he is going to get and he lives the life of dishonesty in the public. The dishonesty can be seen everywhere in the public. The first load of the dishonesty is the political scenario. Our social group has become fed up with the fat, displeasing and money sucking politician. The honest politicians are being thrown out by the money sucking politicians. The law and order is only on a piece of paper. The second road of dishonesty is the backward of the Indian society. Although the literacy levels have improved, yet our rural and semi-urban masses remain illiterate, backward and prone to manipulations. This also causes dishonesty in public life. Keeping in view the above, it can be said that the evils of money took its birth. Man has become dishonest and left aside the time-tested value of life like truth, goodness,

honesty, beauty of mind, body and spirit, charity, hospitality and straight forwardness. The man's aim in today's life is to make money. He can do everything for money. He can make people fool, misguide them, charging more prices etc.. As we all are aware that for getting the work done in all government sectors, one has to follow the method of undertable method. In case if anybody do not follow the method, then his work would not be done. Time and again he was told that your work is in progress or the person who is dealing with the subject is on leave. Finally his work will not be done inspite of wasting money in daily ups and downs. Now it has become very difficult but not impossible to eliminate the dishonesty in public life. For this everybody has to wake up and has to perform his duties honestly.

✓ **(b) Traffic-jams** ⇒ Traffic gridlock has become a daily feature of city life here. While it is an inevitable part of any big city, it has dire consequences in wastage of working hours and increased pollution. The widening of roads and the installation of traffic lights at key junctions has gone some way in making things better on the roads. Complaints about the signal system have been there, but as soon as the system is properly synchronised and additional lights installed at important locations, traffic flow will smoothen out. But alongside the lights, the roads on which they are fitted have to be widened to four lane status, so that separate lanes can be used to prevent traffic jams at junctions. The widening of the Daula Kuan, Safdarjung crossing and introducing flyovers are some of the steps in the right direction. Another essential project is to construct multi story parking lots at strategic places to alleviate the lack of parking space in the city. The parking space should be on a Build-Operate-Transfer(BOT) basis as ample space is available for construction. A final element in the traffic solution would be the completion of the eight lane road under construction on NH-8.

The International Airport lies high on the list of the city's woes. By far the busiest airport in Delhi, which near to Dwarka where number of societies are under construction.

Public transport is a major question for any city, so too here. Currently, only DTC and private buses ply on the roads. These sometimes prove inadequate. A stream lined metro service using buses designed for short trips and easy embarkation-disembarkation is required. A move has already been made by introducing Metro train from Rithala to Shahdara. The metro train could not lead to any hassles with public transport. And the setting up of a second Metro train route is another welcome step. We all know the beneficial effect of the second entrance between Connaught Place and Dwarka station. Now a days, the main reason for traffic congestion is due to construction work carried out for laying pillars for introduction of metro train on different routes. The contractor has acquired lot of space on the road for digging and carrying out the works leaving a small passage on many roads which lead to traffic jams. The other aspect of traffic jam is increase in number of vehicles plying on road. At present most of the people have their own vehicles. The another step in progress to reduce congestion is the metro links between Delhi University to I.S.B.T. and the way from ISBT to Connaught Place is in progress. The another thing of traffic congestion is that there is no proper system of traffic control, growing population and large number of vehicles operating on the road.

✓ **(c) The value of books ⇒** In the forty-plus years, I have been associated with libraries, I thought I had seen and heard all there was concerning the value of books. Foremost is to promote reading and, perhaps, elevate the cultural level of customers. But even more interesting is the premise that books and reading will reduce crime in the subways and, it is also said, "change attitudes and help people get along better."

I am confident, however, that books can and do change the way people think and act toward others. This exhibit, now in its fourth year, offers abundant testimony that books have the power to change people's lives for the better. It is also evident that there is not a specific type of book that needs to be read for inspiration. We have seen fiction, biography, autobiography, psychology, art, history, technical treatises, music, philosophy, and poetry cited as examples of inspirational reading year after year. We also have seen a wide variety in the nationality of authors and the publication dates of books recommended. This tells me that nearly all books hold the potential to inspire someone, and that it is really the ability and desire to read that makes the difference. Promoting that desire and ability are motivating factors for the university libraries. It is our hope that the exhibit may, in some way, encourage its viewers to read not only the books recommended, but others as well.

Most of all, I thank the contributors who have shared the insights and feelings about the books that have influenced them. I am confident that some of the books read on the daily commute will inspire their readers to new goals and better lives. The books are the ocean of knowledge. The thorough reading of any knowledgeable book can widen the scopes of the success of a man. It is also said that books are a mans' best friends. If anyone leaves a person during his time of struggle, books will always support him. That is the gift of books to readers.

✓ **(d) A bad neighbour ⇒** Whenever we purchase or live in a house, our life to some extent depends on neighbours. If you get good neighbours, then the day-to-day lives will be smooth, easy and tension free. If we get bad neighbours then our lives will be full of problems, tensions and become uncomfortable. It is also correct to say that it is not only restricted to persons but for all the people over the world and even for the countries. As you are aware, Pakistan is like our next door neighbour but everybody knows that it is our good or bad neighbour. Our country is mainly suffering from its day to day activities. Here I am also quoting an example of bad neighbour. A 24-year-old man stunned police detectives in Rajasthan, as he narrated how he connived with four others to rob his next door neighbour. But , Shri Rajesh who claims to be an auto mechanic, says he committed the evil act under the influence of alcohol. The police, however dismissed his excuse as an act of comedy geared towards whipping up sympathy do cover up his unkind cut against his neighbour, who had been more of a brother to him They are very close neighbours. I have not robbed him. The robbery is not my business. I am a mechanic and it is due to excessive drinking. When he was in police net, he said that he is full of regrets, and has vowed not to go near alcohol if he eventually regains freedom. "I have seen the bad luck of drinking and I won't take it again. This incident is the handiwork of the devil," he lamented.

If you get good an reliable neighbour then you can easily do number of works without any tension. You can left your children with him, go to market for shopping and even can handover the keys of the house. A good neighbour also helps in case of any emergency or need in the mid night or so while a bad neighbour will always think how to hurt your happy life, think of your harm and will jealous with your achievements. He will always think of negative against you. One should avoid these short of bad characteristics so that he could not be called as a bad neighbour.

Q6. Write a dialogue of about 150 words between yourself and your friend on any *one* of the following : [10]

(a) Match-fixing in cricket

(b) TV advertisements

(c) Women's place is in the home

(d) Old age is a curse.

(a) Match-fixing in cricket

Myself : Hello, Pawan, how are you and where were you ?

Pawan : Hello, I am fine and due to my illness, I was on leave and I have joined today only, how are you?

Myself : I am also fine. Do you know that cricket now a days is at its highest level of popularity and is at top of all games, not only in India but also in the world.

Pawan : Yes, it is the most popular game in the world.

Myself : Pawan, the recent happening of match fixing incidents have discouraged its popularity and have brought a bad name.

Pawan : I have heard about the match fixing scandals coming up in the news now a days. It is really a matter of shame. I was just surprised to listen this news.

Myself : You might be knowing that top most cricketers of the team are involved in this scandal and they are also found guilty.

Pawan : Now there is sufficient evidence available against them.

Myself : I do not know, inspite of getting more than enough money, not only from cricket, but from advertisements also , how can our cricketers do this.

Pawan : Now a days the cricketers want to generate more money, whether it is from advertisements, match or match-fixing. They have become greedy.

Myself : Some people are of the opinion that cricket should be banned.

Pawan : It should not be banned but the players found guilty of match fixing should be punished or debarred forever from playing cricket.

Myself : Your suggestion is good but I think it should be banned because it is a waste of time and money, people are mad after cricket. They do not do any work during the matches. A lot of money is wasted, after all what is the use of cricket.

Pawan : If you think so, then every thing should be banned, which is not useful. Basically, it is a source of entertainment.

(b) TV advertisements

Myself : Hello, Pawan, How are you and where were you?

Pawan : Hello, I was on leave and I have joined today only, how are you?

Myself : I am also fine. Where were you ?

Pawan : I have gone to Mumbai for watching one advertisement film made for our company.

Myself : Are you not seeing the advertisements advertised on T.V. ?

Pawan : TV is a worthy media of advertisement now-a-days. For introducing and trading a new product in the market, one has to make its publicity. For the publicity of the products TV is the best media.

Myself : You are right. Now the trend in TV advertisement totally depends on big stars, as big star in a product's advertisement will be more effective.

Pawan : Yes, it can be seen in number of advertisements that are being displayed on TV; for example in Coca Cola advertisement "Aamir Khan" is there, in Thumps up "Salman Khan", in Pepsi we can see "Rithik Roshan".

Myself : Ya, big companies are spending more money in advertisements and taking big stars. Big Multi National Companies like LG, Honda, Fort, Icon etc. are even taking big cricketers like Sachin Tandulkar, Sourav Ganguly, Rahul

Dravid. Among them Sachin Tandulkar is the most demandable person.

Pawan : It is also seen that the income of TV authorities is mainly from advertisements.

Myself : Yes, you are right. They are giving advertisements more in between the serial being shown.

Pawan : The style of advertisement on TV has considerably changed as compared to the past. Some advertisements are very attractive, comical and knowledgeable.

Myself : Pawan, it is also seen that some advertisements are very initiative.

(c) Women's place is in the home

Myself : Hello, Pawan, how are you ?

Pawan : I am fine and what about you.

Myself : I am also fine. Would you please tell me about "Woman's place in the home"

Pawan : A woman has numerous places in house, sometimes she act as a wife, sometimes as a mother, sometimes as a daughter and sometimes as daughter-in-law. All the needs of the family are being taken care of by her.

Myself : There are still some places where woman does not get that much of regard and place in home.

Pawan : Yes, you are right. This is due to slackness in our social system. Generally, most of the people think that woman is a thing meant for use only.

Myself : Many woman are doing very well in their homes only.

Pawan : Yes, they are involving themselves in many works, like teaching, knittng and making household goods etc.

Myself : It is true. The situation has considerably improved but still everybody need to be broad minded, so as to provide a better place to woman in the home.

Pawan : In today's world, people are doing well towards education and giving full respect to the woman.

Myself : It is also seen that in a family where woman is given due respect, that family do not face problems and the family continues to perform well.

Pawan : Well, it is true to some extent. Sometimes what happened, when a woman receives due respect, then she does not bother for anybody and do whatever she likes.

Myself : It happens very rarely.

Pawan : Yes. I also advise that woman should be given due place in the home.

(d) Old age is a curse

Myself : Hello, Pawan, How are you?

Pawan : I am fine and what about you ?

Myself : I am also fine. Do you know that when people become old, it becomes a curse ?

Pawan : Yes, I know. It is only due to their inability to perform works. Because of age factor, they are not having so much of potential in their body to perform any type of work. That is why they are sometimes being ignored by the family members.

Myself : Their own family members are the reason behind it. The family members do not pay much regard and attention to the old people in their house, who are their father grand father, uncle etc.

Pawan : It is really surprising and a matter of disgrace that we are not paying due attention and respect towards our old parents.

Myself : The children forget that a time will come when they will also attain the same age.

Pawan : Yes, it is correct. They do not bother but it is a fact that whenever they attain the old age, they will also face the same difficulty which they are giving to their old parents.

Myself : Due to the old age and ignorance of old parents, they become totally ineffective.

Pawan : They generally lose their confidence of working ability, that is why they are unable to work.

Myself : It is also seen that many people send their old parents to the old age homes.

Pawan : It should be our endeavour to provide them due respect and sufficient time, so that they do not feel lonely and helpless.

Myself : Yes, we should.

Pawan : If we provide them due respect and keep away to understand them as alone, we too will also get the same respect from our children in old age, who are watching the entire episode.

CS-610 FOUNDATION COURSE IN ENGLISH FOR COMPUTING
DEC 2001

Note: *Answer all the questions.*

Q1. Read the passage given below carefully and answer the questions which are based on it :

Scientists in many parts of the world are now trying to reclaim the desert lands. In Iraq, with its two great rivers, everyone thinks straight way of irrigation. Actually, irrigation is not a very important means of reclaiming desert lands. In the first place, only a small part of the world's desert land is near enough to large rivers for men to be able to use them, and in the second place, irrigation itself can be dangerous for the land, where a hot sun evaporates great quantities of water everyday. In fact, irrigation may change fertile land to barren land, and indeed is doing so all the time. The reason for this is simple. All river water is slightly salty (all the sea's salt has been carried into it by the rivers). If we spread river water over the land, and allow it to evaporate we spread salt over, the land too. If we go on doing this, the land becomes so saline that it produces nothing but palm trees and eventually, not even palm trees grow there; the land has become desert.

(i) Choose from the passage the word which means : [6]

(a) salty

(b) to change liquid into vapour

(c) to call back into use

(d) fruitful

(e) to spread water over the land

(f) in the end.

(a) Salty - Saline

(b) to change liquid into vapour - evaporate

(c) to call back into use - reclaim

(d) fruitful - futile/useful

(e) in the end - eventually.

(ii) Why does everyone think of reclaiming desert land in Iraq? [2]

Everyone thinks of reclaiming the desert lands in Iraq because of its two great rivers for irrigation purposes.

(iii) When does a piece of land become desert? [2]

A piece of land becomes desert, when a salty water is continuously spread over it for a long time. The land becomes so saline that eventually it produces nothing and becomes desert.

(iv) How can irrigation at times change fertile land into barren land? [2]

Irrigation at times change fertile land into barren land due to continuous use of slightly salty water of rivers who carried sea's salt. If we spread river water all over the land, and allow it to evaporate we spread salt over the land too. If we go on doing this, the land becomes so saline that it produces nothing and becomes desert.

(v) Give the word opposite in meaning to the words given below and use the new words in sentences of your own : [3]
(a) many
(b) dangerous
(c) simple

(a) Many - few
Few countries were with American War against Iraq.
(b) Dangerous - safe
Any sort of quarrel is not safe for people.
(c) simple - complex
All foreign languages are too complex to understand easily.

Q2. Do as directed : [5]
(a) Switzerland is ________European country
(insert an appropriate article)
(b) They ought to be here _________now.
(fill in the blank with the correct preposition)
(c) Peter has a computer that _________fit into his jacket pocket.
(fill in the blank with an appropriate modal)
(d) "I grew these carrots myself," said Ram.
(Change into reported speech)
(e) John is resembling his older sister.
(correct the error in this sentence)

(a) a
(b) by
(c) may
(d) Ram said that he had grown those carrots himself.
(e) John resembles his elder sister.

Q3. Fill in the blanks with the correct form of the verb given in the brackets: [5]

(a) I __________ at the University for over fifteen years now. (work)

(b) The public _____ requested not to walk on the grass. (be)

(c) With this promotion, I feel that I ——— a turning point in my career. (reach)

(d) He ________(leave) for office before I ______(go) to see him.

(a) have been working.

(b) is

(c) have reached

(d) had left / went

Q4. Rewrite the following in passive voice : [5]

(a) I conducted the test in the school library to minimise noise.

(b) I hope they will have completed all the markings by tomorrow.

(c) The doctor advised me to give up sweets.

(d) They are installing the new computer next month

(e) The committee called in Sarita to explain her reasons for the proposed changes.

(a) The test was conducted by me in the school library to minimise noise.

(b) It is hoped by me that all the markings will have been completed by them by tomorrow.

(c) I was advised by the doctor to give up sweets.

(d) The new computer is being installed by them next month.

(e) Sarita was called in by the committee to explain her reasons for the proposed changes.

Q5. Write a composition in about 200-250 words on any one of the following topics : [10]

(a) Helping the handicapped

(b) Joint families are impractical

(c) Newspaper - Reading

(d) Earthquakes

✓ **(a) Helping the handicapped ⇒** Handicapped can be helped in many ways. Some people liberally give money for their rehabilitation. Central and State Governments are also providing reservation quota for the handicapped in schools, colleges and jobs. Though this is a big direction of their rehabilitation, a large number of population still remains uncaring and unattended even by their parents or relatives. Generally, rich individuals or public trusts provide monetary help which help handicapped to a large extent. But money is not everything, they need most is the affection of parental love and acceptance in

society. Generally we find that the handicapped are looked down by the people at large. They are made objects and laugh on them. This insensitive attitude of the people towards the handicapped breaches their confidence. This develops a complex among them and their progress is further closed up. For those who are not helping the handicapped financially for their rehabilitation, should help them by building their confidence. There are two types of the handicapped, physically challenged and mentally challenged. The condition of the mentally challenged is worse. The condition of the children particularly in this category is even more miserable.
Some voluntary organizations are doing excellent work to rehabilitate the physically and mentally challenged people. The organisations can be helped by donating or adopting any of the boy or girl.

We fulfill our mission of rehabilitation to some extent in the following ways :

- Assisting with medical care by providing medicines, physiotherapy and surgical operations
- Providing wheelchairs and other physical aids.
- Adapting facilities to make them more handicapped friendly.
- Increasing the awareness of the local community about the problems of the handicapped.
- Getting handicapped children in school by providing the necessary support that they need.
- Helping the handicapped to become more independent through job training and support. This primary is done through selling and promoting handicrafts that they make.

✓ **(b) Joint families are impractical ⇒** From the ancient time in Indian society, the concept of joint families have been followed and liked by society. A joint family consists of a head who rules over a large family consisting of brothers, sons, son-in-laws, grandsons, nephews, daughters, daughter-in-laws and so on. This concept is still being followed in the rural India. But these days, with the growing cities, education, expanding industries, shrinking land holdings, the concept of joint family has almost collapsed in the urban and semi urban families in India. The needs of those times evolved the joint family system. In ancient time, it was not possible for an individual or two to withstand the violences of nature, epidemics or any other crisis. Man made and nature created problems were being collectively faced by the people, i.e. agriculture need collective effort. Also the work of carpenters, mistri etc. could not be performed without the collective effort of the people. Therefore, to avoid any economic or social problem, people did everything jointly as a community and the family members lived together to earn their livelihood. So,

the joint family system was a necessity at that time. With the introduction of industrial revolution the need of the people changed. The families in the villages began to migrate to the cities for doing jobs in the factories or private concerns and they left their joint families and settled down in the towns for better prospects. Industrialisation also created the need of education in the common people. It is also seen that members of the joint families came in the cities for higher education. It is seen that at present the system of joint families is completely blown. People become more interested in their own progress and welfare and they do not bother about the other family members. Also the members do not want to share any responsibility of other family members and want to enjoy their prosperity without any body's disturbance.
In today's world, the nature of man has totally changed. He does not want anybody's interference in his family life. He becomes selfish and limited to his own family only. He even does not bother about other members of his family. At present the system of joint families is disappearing day by day.

(c) Newspaper - Reading
Please Refer to DEC02, Q5(c)

(d) Earthquakes
Please Refer to JUNE02, Q6(iii)

Q6. Write a dialogue in about 150 words between A and B on any one of the following : [10]
(a) A tells B (his friend) about a strange dream he had.
(b) A asks B for directions to the Public Library.
(c) A telephones B for dinner.
(d) A and B are passengers in a bus and they get talking.

(a) A tells B (his friend) about a strange dream he had
Please Refer to DEC03, Q6(b)

(b) A asks B for directions to the Public Library
A - Sir, may I trouble you ?
B - Why not, it will be my pleasure if I would be able to guide you.
A - Sir, I am a student doing B.C.A. from correspondence. I need some guidance from you. Our university is having a very small library and sufficient number of books are not available. I want to go through some reference books.
B - What do you want from me? Can I tell you the name and author of reference books.

A - Sir, I am in need of your guidance. I will be very grateful if you guide me for a library, which is having sufficient number of books and I can sit and study for hours together.

B - You can join Delhi Public Library. It is an excellent library. You could sit there from morning till evening quietly and could do your studies.

A - Does it contain sufficient number of all kind of books?

B - Yes, you will get books of your choice and it is nearly two kilometers away from here.

A - For joining the library, what are the formalities needed ?

B - It is very easy. You have to bring your recent passport size photograph along with identity card of your college or ration card. Their charges are also very nominal.

A - Sir, could you guide me the way to the Delhi Public Library, I would like to register my name today only.

B - Well, I am sure you will reach there very comfortably.

A - If the road leading to library is good then I would like to go on foot otherwise I will take a rickshaw.

B - If it was nearer then I would definitely accompany you, but it is two kilometers away from here and I cannot walk so much.

A - You please guide me, Sir, I will manage to go there.

B - First, you have to take a right turn from that red light and go straight. After walking few steps, you will find a well furnished restaurant. From that restaurant take a left turn and go to the extreme end of the road. At the end of the road you will find one big sign board depicting 'Way to Delhi Public Library' and that is your Library.

A : Sir, Thank you very much for extending me such a nice cooperation. I am very grateful to you. Thanking you once again.

(c) A telephones B inviting him for dinner

A - Hello, May I speak to Mr. B.

B - May I know who is on the line ?

A - I am A on the line.

B - Hello Mr. A where were you, I have tried your telephone a number of times but could not contact you.

A - How are you ?

B - I am fine here and hope you will also be fine there.

A - Yah, I am also fine here.

B - Mr. A, everything is all-right.

A - What happened ? Why are you asking this question ?

B - I have asked this question only because you have called me after a gap of six months.

A - Really. If so, sorry, please forgive me.

B - There is no need of sorry. Anyway tell me what are you doing at present?

A - After doing graduation, I joined papa and had a long training with him. Now, I am associated my father in his business. What are you doing ?

B - After completing my graduation, I got a job in Income Tax Department and I am continuing the same.

A - Good, I am very glad to hear.

B - Now tell me what is the matter ?

A - As you are aware, that I am having one sister Rama. She is going to be married soon and we are arranging a small dinner party in Hotel Ramniwas where my sister and her fiance both would be there. You are cordially invited to attend the dinner party and be with us along with your family members.

B - Thanks for remembering me. I accept your invitation and will definitely attend the party. Please convey my regards and congratulate her.

A - Thanks. We are meeting tomorrow at Hotel Ramniwas. Bye.

B - Bye.

(d) A and B are passengers in a bus and they get talking

A - Excuse me, is this seat vacant.

B - Yes, it is vacant and you can sit.

A - Sir, where are you going ?

B - I am going to Rai Breilly and you.

A - I am going to Muradabad.

B - Muradabad ! That means that half the way we are together.

A - I will enjoy your company.

B - You are going to Muradabad for what ?

A - I am going to Muradabad for meeting my family. My family is basically from Muradabad.

B - When did you turn up from there ?

A - I am a student and generally I visit there on Saturday and holidays.

B - Every holiday ?

A - Most of the holidays I spent with my family.

B - In which college are you studying ?

A - Birla Institute of Technology. I am doing my business management from there.

B - It is really a nice college.

A - It is one of the good colleges in Kerala and what about you ?

B - You are a student while I was a student in Kerala Vidhyanagar. I am moving over there for my certificates. The student life has now been completed and we are now in the market.

A - How do you feel after completing your studies ?
B - Feel to be complete but a good job will make me more happy.
A - You are looking for a job ?
B - At present, I am on training in a company but soon will be in a good position in the same company.
A - Same one or might be some other then. Thanks for the company, bye.
B - Bye. See you soon.

CS-610 FOUNDATION COURSE IN ENGLISH FOR COMPUTING
JUNE 2002

Note: *Attempt all the questions.*

Q1. Read the passage given below carefully and answer the questions which are based on it:

You know that fluids exert pressure equally in all directions. This fact is important to human beings, for the pressure of the atmosphere is 1034 kilograms per square centimetre, which, if it were exerted in one direction only would crush us all to death.

It is amazing to think that this basic fact was discovered comparatively recently -- in the 17th century- by an Italian Teuricelli. He had discovered, as many had before him that no pump could suck up water from a greater depth than 9.7 meters. He reasoned that it must be because the pressure of the atmosphere was equal to the weight of the column of water of that height. He therefore took a liquid much heavier than water, mercury and filled an open-ended tube with it and stood it in a bowl of mercury. The mercury dropped until it stood about 76 cm above the level in the bowl. The basic concept of atmospheric pressure and its behaviour was confirmed by Pascal: who showed that the level of mercury in the tube fell when it was taken up a mountain, thus establishing a clear relationship between height and pressure.

It was later discovered that variations in pressure are indicative of changes in weather - a fall in pressure indicates bad weather.

(i) Say whether the following statements are true or false:

(a) The fact that air exerts pressure was discovered 300 years ago.

(b) A pump cannot suck water from a greater depth than 9.7 metres because water exerts pressure downwards.

(c) The heavier the liquid used in a barometer the smaller the height of will be the column of the liquid in the barometer.

(d) The pressure of the atmospheric air on a mountain is lower.

(e) Fluids exert pressure only downwards.

(a) True
(b) False
(c) False
(d) True
(e) False

(ii) Way does pressure of atmosphere not crush us to death? [2]

The pressure of atmosphere does not crush us to death because the fluids exert pressure equally in all directions in the atmosphere.

(iii) Choose from the passage the word which means **[4]**

(a) surprising

(b) not long ago

(c) primary

(d) changes

(a) Surprising - amazing

(b) not long ago - recently

(c) primary - basic

(d) changes - variations.

(iv) Write a summary of the passage. **[3]**

Fluids exert pressure in all directions. The pressure of the atmosphere is 1034 kilograms per square centimeter and if it were exerted in one direction only would crush us all to death. It is amazing to note that this basic fact was discovered comparatively recently in the 17th century by an Italian Teuricelli, it was that no pump could suck up water from a greater depth than 9.7 meters because the pressure of the atmosphere was equal to the weight of the column of water of that height. He took an open-ended tube filled with mercury, heavier than water and stood it in a bowl of mercury. The mercury dropped until it stood about 76 cm above the level in the bowl. The basic concept of atmospheric pressure and its behaviour was given by Pascal establishing a clear relationship between height and pressure. It was later discovered that variations in pressure are indicative of changes in weather - a fall in pressure indicates bad weather.

Q2. Fill in the blanks with the correct forms of the verbs: **[5]**

(i) My mother and I___________ tea every morning. (drink)

(ii) I__________ my dinner an hour ago. (have)

(iii) My father___________ seventy years old last Tuesday. (be)

(iv) The child___________ very much since I last________ her. (grow, see)

(i) drink

(ii) had

(iii) had been

(iv) has grown, saw

Q3. Rewrite the following in passive voice [4]
(i) Someone washes old plastic bottles and then someone crushes them.
(ii) Who will open the gate in his absence?
(iii) We expect good news.
(iv) Who will help her children now?

(i) Old plastic bottles are washed by someone and then crushed by someone.
(ii) By whom the gate would be opened in his absence?
(iii) Good news are expected.
(iv) By whom now her children would be helped?

Q4. Do as directed: [7]
(i) He is__________ FBI agent (Insert a suitable article)
(ii) If he had all the wealth in the world____________ (complete the sentence)
(iii) I told him that he couldn't hope to catch a big fish____________ a small rod like that, but he insisted typing
(Fill in the blanks with appropriate prepositions)
(iv) "Way isn't Tim here yet?" "It______________ be because his mother is ill again."
(Fill in the blank with an appropriate modal)
(v) Each buses owned by the company are washed once a week.
(Correct the sentence)
(vi) Uncle Ram is a very jolly person, be he is full of ________
(fun, joke)
(Fill in the blank space by inserting whichever of the alternatives given you think is the correct one)

(a) a
(ii) he would have completed his world tour.
(iii) by, on
(iv) would
(v) Each bus owned by the company is washed once a week.
(vi) fun

Q5. Change the following sentences into reported speech: [2]
(a) Shiela said, "It gives me great pleasure to be here this evening."
(b) He said, "Be quiet and listen to my words."

(a) Sheila told that it gave her great pleasure to be there that evening.
(b) He ordered to be quiet and listen to his words.

Q6. Write a composition in about 200 words on any *one* of the following: [10]

(i) Travelling and its educational value
(ii) Clean surroundings help to prevent diseases
(iii) Earthquakes - a national calamity
(iv) The book you like most

✓ **(i) Travelling and its educational value ⇒** The value of education on travelling plays a very important role in making out a programme. If anybody wants to make a trip, the first step is what type of management skills would be required. The step to learn is about the one of preparations and packing. It is really difficult to manage things. We must decide about the most essential articles to carry i.e. first aid kit, survival kit having important tools, clothes, entertainment items and small hand bags. These are the bare necessities which one must carry with him. As the transportation of baggage is scarce and costly, it is more beneficial to carry items which are conveniently transported. Travel with a group imparts lessons in human interaction and team work. The members of the group can share tasks according to their capacities and training. As can be seen that some people are experts in arranging tickets and transport, some in map-reading and some in acting as translators in regions where different languages are spoken.

Whatever be the means of journey, people get unknown experiences which enrich them. People in the past could not travel because of inadequate means of transportation. Their cultures were introvert and scattered. They looked at foreigners with fear and hate. In today's world, travelling has become very easy. We can travel all over the world and can avail the fastest mode of transportation like by air, by sea or even by road. To sum up, we must go on a world tour for imparting unknown experiences.

(ii) Clean surroundings help to prevent diseases

Please Refer to DEC04, Q6(ii).

✓ **(iii) Earthquakes - a national calamity ⇒** It is true that earthquakes are a national calamity. Catastrophes such as earthquakes can happen suddenly and cause massive destruction. Some people think that calamity is just bad luck, while others seek out reasons for their misfortune.

Earthquakes are difficult to predict and often impossible to prevent. The calamities are rooted in human psychology and may be even more difficult to prevent.

Gujrat on 26th January, 2001 came in close contact with the most inspiring horror of natural disasters of our nation, when Indian people were watching the Republic Day Parade on their television sets.

Recently, on 29th December, 2004, the south of little Andaman and west coast of Indonesia have experienced two moderate intensity earthquakes. A moderate

intensity earthquake, measuring 5.1 on Richter scale, occurred at around 22:41 hrs with an epicentre at 10.1 degree north latitude and 92.8 degree east longitude near the south of Little Andaman.
The epicentre of the other quake, which measured 5.3 on the Richter scale, was 4.5 degree north latitude and 94.5 degree east longitude near west coast of Indonesia and occurred at around 20:19 hours yesterday.
Sri Lanka has suffered large scale damage and devastation as a result of the tsunami disaster. Media reports indicate that over 10,000 people are dead, with thousands more injured and missing. Many are displaced from their homes as a result of the disaster. Due to the scale of the devastation, (affected areas range from the North through East to the South and also the West), reaching those in need is a difficult task. Immediate needs are food, clothing and drinking water. Water treatment material is a major priority as sea water has contaminated the drinking water sources, such as wells.
Medicine for minor sicknesses and injuries is also urgently needed, as well as food for the displaced who are at various centres, such as churches and other places of worship.
As sea has not yet fully settled, people have been advised not to return to their areas of former residence. Many however, have no houses to go back to. They have lost all their earthly belongings.

✓ **(iv) The book you like best ⇒** The likings differ from man to man, some like playing, some like cooking, some like eating, some like wondering here and there but I like reading books the most. There are different kind of books like novels, stories, educational books etc.. I always like to read educational books. By reading books you can not only increase your knowledge but also can spend your time in an excellent manner. Whenever you get a book of your choice, then you can't imagine when the time has past. I also want to advise everyone of a most interesting book I read last year : The Myth of Male Power, by Warren Farrel, Ph.D. He was once a member of the National Organisation of Women (NOW) board of directors, but he became disenchanted with the anti-male bias at now and resigned. One of the most interesting facts he presents in this book is that most statistics on domestic violence come from police reports. Most such reports are made by women against men. This makes sense, because few men who sustain physical attacks by their wives or girlfriends bother to call the cops. I know this is true, because I used to be a cop. On the other hand, I also know—again because I used to be a cop—that women do attack men frequently, and those cases which come to police attention are usually called in by neighbours, or by hospital emergency room personnel due to extensive injuries or the involvement of weapons.
In other words, hospital records reveal that an equal percentage of men are

battered by female domestic partners as are women battered by male domestic partners?

Anyway, I highly recommend this book. It's very readable, and contains many other fascinating facts and statistics. Also interesting book can prove to be useful like a friend.

Q7. Write a dialogue in about 200 words on any *one* of the following: [8]

(i) A customer and a shopkeeper selling books
(ii) Geeta telephones Sita telling her that she will not be able to attend her party
(iii) John and lqbal discuss holiday plans
(iv) Heena and Rama talk about life in a big city

(i) Customer : Hello, is it Education Book Depot ?
Shopkeeper : Yes, Sir, you are right. What can I do for you ?
Customer : I want some books.
Shopkeeper : Which books, Sir.
Customer : Do we have books on Spiritual Knowledge written by Shri Jagdish Chander and of Accounts written by Prof. B.S. Shukla.
Shopkeeper : Yes, we have.
Customer : What are the prices ?
Shopkeeper : The first one is costing Rs.120/- and the other Rs.160/-. We are providing 30% discount on all books on the eve of New Year till January, 2005.
Customer : What are your business timings and also guide me how can I reach your shop from Dhaula Kuan.
Shopkeeper : Our timings are from 10:00 hrs.to 19:00 hrs. with Sunday closed. You can take a bus from Dhaula Kuan and take a ticket upto Pahar Ganj. After dropping at Pahar Ganj, you just see in opposite direction. There is a board where the name of our shop is written. You may not feel any difficulty in locating our shop.
Customer : Oh, your shop is in Pahar Ganj. One of my friend is very much in Pahar Ganj. I will contact and direct him to purchase the books from your shop for me.
Shopkeeper : OK, Sir would you like to buy any other book?
Customer : Do you have any new editions on the above subject written by any author.
Shopkeeper : Yes, we have. The latest edition on the subject has been written by Shri Goyanka Choudhury. It is good book and is in very much demand, that is why we have procured fifty copies of this book.
Customer : What is the price of this book ?

Shopkeeper : It is little bit costly. It is costing Rs.150/- and discount will remain the same.

Customer : OK, then you give this book to him also. My friend will contact you and give my reference. My name is Ram.

Shopkeeper : OK, Sir, I have noted down your name and as and when anybody contact me by giving your reference, the books will be handed over to him on payment. Anything else, sir ?

Customer : No, thanks !

Shopkeeper : You are most welcome, Sir.

(ii) Geeta : Hello, May I speak to Sita, please ?

Sita : Yes, I am Sita speaking. May I know your good name please?

Geeta : Hi, please try to recognise.

Sita : Sorry, I don't remember.

Geeta : I am Geeta here.

Sita : Hi, sorry I could not recognize your voice.

Geeta : Wish you a very very happy wedding anniversary.

Sita : Thank you very much but it will not suffice the purpose. I have arranged a small party and you have to come in the party along with all family members.

Geeta : Definitely, your gift is also ready. How are the preparations for the party going on ? Can I assist you ?

Sita : Thanks, everything has been well organized. Your help will be your presence in the party.

Geeta : Probably I would not be able to attend your party. I am sorry.

Sita : Oh no, anything wrong with you.

Geeta : My brother has fallen ill and nobody from our family is at home, so I have to look after him.

Sita : Is there any serious problem ?

Geeta : Nothing much. As you are aware, he is a heart patient and has got trouble since last night. The entire episode is due to gastic problem to him.

Sita : Have you gone to a doctor for checking up?

Geeta : Yes, doctor says that it is just gas trouble and some medicines have also been given for speedy recovery.

Sita : In case of any emergency, don't hesitate to contact me. I am always at your service.

Geeta : Sure, I would contact you in case of any serious problems. But I am sorry that I would not be able to attend the party.

Sita : Hey, do not feel sorry. First is the health of your brother, take care of him. We will enjoy it next time.

Geeta : Thank you very much and once again wish you a very happy wedding aniversary.

(iii) John : Hi Iqbal, how are you ?
Iqbal : Hi John, I am fine. How are you ?
John : I am also fine. How was your paper ?
Iqbal : The paper was little difficult but I have performed well.
John : How is life going on ?
Iqbal : After examination life has become very humdrum because I have not any work to do and number of holidays are ahead.
John : Oh, this means that you are having number of holidays, so why don't you join any computer course or undergo any training during the holidays.
Iqbal : I have worked very hard for the preparation of the said paper, now I want to relax.
John : Do you have any plan, if so, please tell me.
Iqbal : This time I want to use my holidays in a good manner.
John : You want to utilize your holidays in which sense.
Iqbal : I am talking about moving to some place, to some new atmosphere. Also there are number of packages available from different tour operators. I will pick one of them and enjoy.
John : It will cost you more. If you don't mind, I will suggest you to go to camp
Iqbal : Camp ? Where ? and When ?
John : Just wait. You have raised too many questions at a time. As you may be aware that youth club arranges camp trip during the holidays. They take to mountain areas like Abu, Kulu-Manali, Shimla.
Iqbal : How many days ?
John : It entirely depends on your choice. If you choose Abu, it takes 3 to 4 days. Kulu/Manali takes 7 to 8 days and Shimla even more than that. If you are interested, I will inquire. It also depends upon the activities you choose.
Iqbal : Activities ?
John : Activities like mountain climbing, rock climbing, skating, river crossing etc.
Iqbal : I don't have any experience in the above activities. Who will teach me these activities?
John : There would be a group of volunteers of our age group. They would help us everywhere.
Iqbal : You just make inquiries and if possible, make registration.
John : OK, I will check up and let you apprise.
Iqbal : OK, bye bye, see you soon.
John : OH, bye bye, thank you.
(iv) Heena : Hi Rama! glad to see you after such a long time. Where are you?

Rama : Me too. How is life going on ?

Heena : It has been the same as it was before. Are there any changes or progress?

Rama : You see, I have changed a lot and achieved what I want to.

Heena : Yes, life in a metropolitan city is actually great. Looking at you, I could definitely say that progress is in big city only.

Rama : Definitely, one can make his career and life is pleasurable with luxury.

Heena : Do you own a kothi or a flat ?

Rama : The party has provided a luxury flat and a car.

Heena : There must be a traffic problem.

Rama : The major problem in the big city is traffic jam but everything is going on smoothly.

Heena : I do not think there must be a problem of shopping etc.

Rama : There are multistoried buildings both residential as well as commercial. The commercial buildings have both shops as well as offices. One need not to go very far away to buy a thing.

Heena : To live in big city is really fun.

Rama : Definitely. There are multiplexes for movies, parks to play, morning walk or exercise, banks, corporate offices, fun world, big schools and colleges. Almost every facility is available in the city. One has not to go far away or wait for any thing.

Heena : Everything has its own importance. The only thing that one could not get in big cities is purity and peace of mind.

Rama : You are right Heena. For purity and peace of mind one should go to a hill station or a religious place.

Heena : In big cities life is very fast. Since morning till evening everybody is in a hurry.

Rama : Yes. Everybody is travelling in fast mode and nobody cares about others. The vehicles continue to ply on the roads in the night also. Also, most of the people lead a miserable life in a big city.

Heena : Why so?

Rama : Generally these people remain under the influence of liquor and do not work. Their children are also wondering here and there for money.

Heena : OK, Rama, I have wasted your lot of time.

Rama : Don't worry, OK bye bye.

Heena : bye bye. See you soon.

CS-610 : FOUNDATION COURSE IN ENGLISH FOR COMPUTING
DEC 2002

Note: *Attempt all the questions.*

Q1. Read the passage given below and answer the questions which are based on it:

The origin of computer virus is linked to an interesting game programme known as 'Core-War' developed in AT&T's Bell laboratories. This programme worked on the programming concept of 'self-replicating software' and used it to devour rival's programs instead of data. When this interesting programming concept was made public, the programmers got into the act of developing various programs based on this concept, which would penetrate someone else's system and create havoc there. Because of their destructive nature, these programs came to be known as 'viruses or computer viruses'. From then onwards, computer viruses have become a real menace for computer users all over the world.

A computer virus is programmed to reproduce itself very fast and swarm the computer as biological viruses do in a human body. Perhaps the most deadly similarity between the electronic and biological viruses is their tendency to spread. The computer virus does not spread by mere contact of two floppy diskettes or computers, rather the infection occurs mostly through the use of floppy diskettes which are infected by the virus. When you save or copy files to the diskettes, viruses are transferred from one source to the other, thereby, infecting other systems. When they find their way into another computer, they pollute or destroy data, or valuable software and slow down the operation of the computer, or possibly stop its activities.

Other similarities with biological viruses are: 1 - The virus cannot be seen with the naked eye. To locate the virus you would need specialised software called anti-virus software. 2 - You can use the system (software/ hardware or combination) as a vaccine which would protect you when the virus tries to invade the system. Even here, prevention is better than cure.

(i) State whether the following statements are true or false: [5]

(a) The origin of computer virus is biological.

(b) A computer virus is basically a software.

(c) A computer virus unlike a biological virus can be seen with the naked eye.

(d) A computer virus does not spread by mere contact of floppy diskettes.
(e) It is possible to protect the computer from virus.
(a) False
(b) True
(c) False
(d) True
(e) True

(ii) What is a computer virus? **[2]**
A computer virus is a program which is programmed to reproduce itself very fast and swarm the computer as biological viruses do in a human body.

(iii) Why do you think virus is named as virus? **[2]**
Virus is named as virus because of its nature. It has got a destructive nature As biological virus spread through the body and destroy that part of the body, similarly computer virus is spread through the computer and destroy all the data. It penetrates someone's system and creates havoc on that system. Whenever they find their way, they pollute or destroy data, valuable software and slow down the operations of the computer, even at times it stops the activities.

(iv) Give a synonym each for the following words used in the passage: **[3]**
(a) devour
(b) havoc
(c) locate
(a) devour - demolish
(b) havoc - destruction
(c) locate - situate

Q2. Fill in the blanks with the correct form of the verb given in the brackets: **[6]**
(a) Smita ___________ the violin brilliantly. (play)
(b) We __________ London three times last year. (visit)
(c) She __________ since last January. (ill)
(d) When I saw him he _______ chess. (play)
(e) I found out that he _________ guilty. (be)
(f) After the teacher ________ we began shouting. (go)
(a) plays
(b) visited
(c) has been ill

(d) was playing
(e) was
(f) had gone

Q3. Do as directed: **[5]**

(a) The best way to learn a musical instrument is to find ________ enthusiastic teacher. (Insert an article)
(b) The dog ran away from me and disappeared ________ the hill. (Insert a preposition)
(c) He said to me, "I shall go home tomorrow."
(Change into indirect speech)
(d) Sharad is resembling his older sister. (Correct the sentence)
(e) I went to the village
My friend lives there.
(Combine the two sentences into one complex sentence by using an adjective clause)

(a) an
(b) on
(c) He said to me that he will go home next day.
(d) Sharad resembles his elder sister.
(e) I went to the village where my friend lives.

Q4. Rewrite the following in passive voice.
(a) People are destroying large areas of forest.
(b) They saw him climbing over the fence.
(c) I enjoyed taking children to the zoo.
(d) You can play with these cubs quite safely.
(e) They are repairing the bridge.

(a) Large areas of forest are being destroyed by the people.
(b) He was seen by them climbing over the fence.
(c) Taking children to the zoo was enjoyed by me.
(d) The game could not be played by you with these cubs quite safely.
(e) The bridge is being repaired by them.

Q5. Write a composition in about 400 words on any *one* of the following: **[2]**

(a) Entering the world of fantasy with computers
(b) Cyber cafes
(c) Newspaper in education
(d) Terrorism

✓ **(a) Entering the world of fantasy with computers** ⇒ One of the things that "Fantasy Writer" is about the importance of attempting to understand the pleasure others find. As you are aware that there was a time when children are playing video games with a pretty lonely experience in the semi dark room hunched over the computer screen. They are simply playing the games and they do not know the practical fantasy world of the game designer's making. Sometimes they assess themselves as hero in some puzzle-solving and sometimes painful, existence of their ordinary lives. But now all that is changing. Computer applications are not only used for games but also designing cars, trains, aeroplanes and even medical diagnosis of patients. The computers available in the market at present are equipped with the most modern appliances and well versed with applications like E-mail, E-com, internet surfing, multimedia, voice mail, business applications, CAD, CA, entertainment and web cameras. For video games there are number of web sites from where games can be down loaded. An Internet connection and a paid membership to the game's Web sites allow the subscribers to play twenty four hours a day. After installing the games on the computer, the player only needs to create a character to represent himself before entering this new game world.

The other world of fantasy with the computer is the Robots. They are computerized machines equipped with remote sensing devices and can respond according to their surroundings. Robots are generally used for the risky or repetitive works. The another world of fantasy with the computer is of animation and multimedia. The animation has created his own world of fantasy. Many of the stories and fantasy tales had been developed and made out of the creative thinking. Everyone has its own fantasy world in their dream and this dream comes true with computer by animation. A large number of computer games have been Internet and web based games are created which can be played any time at two ends of the world without knowing each other.

✓ **(b) Cyber cafes** ⇒ Cyber cafes are the places where one can use Internet facility independently on paying a nominal amount on hourly basis. The first cyber cafe in India was introduced in Bangalore and at that time the use of Internet on hourly basis is not cheap as now. The first Internet browser was introduced by Mr. Tim Barnes in European Particle Physics Laboratory in the Swiss Alps. This software was a surprising tool and with the help of this we can see documents, photos/video on the Internet. It was named as World Wide Web by users and it is made essential for Information, Communication and Entertainment (ICE). The word 'www' (World Wide Web) is used before the name of every web sites you desire to see. At present the use of Internet has increased considerably and more cyber cafes are required to be opened. Cyber cafes in posh colonies are well furnished with air-conditioning facility and songs or light music goes on. People goes to cyber cafes for surfing the internet, chating etc.. Some are going for down loading educational material from internet. Also some are updating their web sites running on the Internet. Internet is used for booking hotel accommodation, air tickets, railway tickets/ information, education guidance, entertainment, down loading movies etc. It is being used by every category of people. In India there are approximately 5,00,000 Internet subscribers and due to shared users and cyber cafes the total number of users increases to approximately 20,00,000 whereas in USA there are more than 100 million users. As India is one of the lowest telephone connections per capita of any country in the world, only those who can afford these gadgets can conduct internet telephony on their own while others can avail of the facility from cyber cafe. The number of cyber cafes are increasing day by day. They are now available in every street, city and town. In most of the cities cyber cafes have been visited regularly by the people.

Cybercafe has been a saving for the middle class people because they are not able to buy a personal computer or high billed telephone. It is very difficult for them to daily take the advantage of internet. A good solution for them is cybercafe. Cyber Cafe has become a meeting place for the people and they are spending hours over there without any hesitations or risk.

Cyber Cafes are the easy way to work on internet for every people.

✓ **(c) Newspaper in education** ⇒ The word 'NEWS' stands for North, East, West and South. A newspaper, therefore, gives us news from all the four directions daily. Every person, either is a young or an old person, a businessman or a service man, a student and a teacher goes through the newspaper for the news of his or her interest . It updates oneself with the news around the world and even helps out the students to be aware of the current affairs. Newspaper in Education, is an international program begun in 1955 to advance the use of newspapers in schools. The main purpose of the program is to improve reading, spelling and writing abilities.

There is substantial evidence that using newspapers in schools contributes to students' reading skills, writing skills, and current event knowledge. The effects are most dramatic among minorities. Literacy experts believe that adults with low level literacy skills lack a sufficient foundation of basic skills to function successfully in our society. By providing schools with newspapers, sponsors can help prevent illiteracy at time when young people have a support system of educators in place. Newspapers open the world to them and give them a chance to succeed.

Teachers use the newspapers as textbooks and supplements in areas such as reading, writing, maths, science, history, economics, language arts, special education.

Newspapers are considered the most up-to-date, inexpensive textbook available to students. Students can compile a list of words that they are not familiar from the newspaper and can also make a crossword puzzle using these words and definitions that they have researched. A crossword puzzle makes their vocabulary larger. By reading newspaper, the grammar of students can be increased. The skills gained from regular newspaper exposure make each student a better learner, a better problem-solver, and a better leader.

✓ **(d) Terrorism** ⇒ In today's modernistic world, terrorism has become a very severe problem. This menace has especially been faced in India for more than twenty years. Initially it started from Punjab where Amritsar was the place. The Golden temple was brought down by the terror. After then many terrorist activities are taking place in Jammu and Kashmir and surrounding areas. It is understood that Pakistan is having the training camp for such terrorists across the border and many terrorists infiltrate from Pakistan border. Unluckily, the world community has not taken any note of India's sufferings. America wake up for the first time on 11 September, 2001 when the 'World Trade Centre' towers in New York and 'Pentagon' were lashed out. The Taliban Government in Afghanistan was brought down and America declared global war and the Al Qaida men were targetted, who were the activists organized the attacks in America. In 2003, the coalition forces headed by America, attacked Iraq to end the regime but America remained regardless of India's problem with terrorism. The terrorists have not left even temples and mosques. The recent attack was in Akshardham. Kashmir which was known as heaven on earth had become like hell because of terror and threat that continues over there since long period. The modern terrorist attacks are attacks on people representing the whole society. The communication through Internet have made it possible for extremist political organisations to build large organisational networks, exchange information and combine resources. Terrorism in the 21st Century has an impact on people and nations far greater than ever before, using the forces and tools of globalisation which have the ability to spread fear around the globe. Subsequent attacks produced the recognition that no-one is safe wherever they are in the world. Terrorism has become a global problem with global moments. The terrorism has become a global problem with global consequences. Is there an alternative to a war against terrorism in India where millions of people loose their lives, which leaves the children's to live as orphans and in misery, mothers to cry for their sons… Can't the terror among people be killed? Can't a war begin and end without loosing the life of an innocent? Isn't there any stop to terrorism in India? With the hype and media attention surrounding terrorism in the beginning of this century there is sure to be many more reports and books to be published on this matter

Q6. Write a dialogue between your friend and you in about 150 words on any *one* of the following topics: [10]

(a) Your friend Prakash has invited you for a movie. You accept his invitation.

(b) Your friend Asha is of the opinion that watching television is bad for young children. You disagree with her.

(c) You invite your friend Gopal for a picnic but he declines your invitation.

(a) Pramod : Hello, Prakash, how are you ?

Myself : I am fine and what about you ?

Pramod : I am also fine. Where are you at present and what are you doing ?

Myself : At present I am in your city Delhi and doing a Government job.

Pramod : Very good. What are you doing on coming Sunday afternoon ?

Myself : I am doing nothing on the coming Sunday and I may be alone at home because my parents are going outside Delhi. Why are you asking? What is the matter ?

Pramod : As a matter of fact, we friends have planned to watch a movie and I thought that you should also accompany us.

Myself : I will be glad to join you. Who else is going ? Is Rakesh senior also accompanying us ?

Pramod : Ravi, Rakesh, Roshan and myself along with you are planning to watch a movie.

Myself : Very good. I will certainly join you. Which movie are you planning to see? Can I also suggest a movie ?

Pramod : We are planning to see the coloured version of 'Mughal-e-Azam', however, your suggestion is welcome.

Myself : It is very amazing, I too planning to see the coloured version of 'Mughal-e-Azam'. When did you leave for movie from your residence ?

Pramod : Since I have taken the tickets for noon show, we will leave home at 1100 hrs.. We on our way will pick you up from your residence.

Myself : By the way, which threatre are we going to ?

Pramod : 'PVR Plaza' in Connaught Place.

Myself : OK. I will wait for you at my residence. Bye bye, see you.

(b) Asha : In the house television is really an idiot box which is not only spoiling our children's habit but also their future.

Myself : I don't think so. It is a good information provider and entertainer for all of us.

Asha : For children ! I am surprised to hear the above. Children are sitting in front of the television and watching it continuously. Television has made them so lazy that they do not go out for playing.

Myself : Watching television is better than playing outside the entire day.
Asha : How, can you explain me ?
Myself : You do not know with whom the child is playing and how is his company. Children can grasp bad habits faster then good habits.
Asha : They are not free for the entire day. They go to school, do their homework, go to attend tuition classes.
Myself : So, in another word, they have no time to enjoy. They may be given time to enjoy their childhood. Television provides them entertainment and many educational channels. They can see cartoons, discovery channel etc. who take them to the world of fantasy.
Asha : There are number of channels and we do not know which programme is being shown on TV. Immoral programs and nudity mainly affects on their immature mind.
Myself : It is entirely in our hand to let them see the informatory programs and skillful serials. As mentioned above, cartoon programs take them to the world of fantasy, which make them originative. Programs displayed on discovery channel and quiz provide them worthy information beyond the world. There are number of family serials shown on Star Plus and Sony TV which inspire them to recognise family values and regard to elders. It cannot be denied that television gives entertainment with knowledge.

(c) Myself : Gopal, wish you a Happy New Year.
Gopal : Kamlesh, I heartily reciprocate the same to you and your family.
Myself : Gopal, on the eve of New Year I along with all my family members are planning for a picnic.
Gopal : All family members you mean to say your brothers, sisters, cousins, mummy, papa and grand pa too.
Myself : Yes, all. Are you free that day or have you planned something?
Gopal : I am free and I have not planned anything yet.
Myself : Why don't you accompany us ?
Gopal : How can I accompany you? You are going with your family.
Myself : My dear friend, everybody knows you and you are like a member of our family.
Gopal : Thanks for remembering me but it is a family picnic. I won't think it will look nice for me to come.
Myself : Hey ! come on dear. Everyone in my family knows you and you are a part of our family. Also I have taken permission from my father.
Gopal : No, dear. You please go, I have some work to do that day.
Myself : Do not make excuses. It has already been decided by us that you are accompanying us for picnic.

Gopal : Kamlesh wait for a minute and listen to me first. I have seriously got some work and I know that if I accompany you everybody in your family would be glad, but the work is also of an urgent nature and needs to be completed.

Myself : I know that now you are making excuses. Actually you do not want to come with us because you are feeling unknown to join us. Please do not feel unknown and join us.

Gopal : I regard your feeling.

Myself : If you will not accompany for picnic then I also will not go.

Gopal : No. You please go. I will promise you that next time I will definitely accompany you.

Myself : OK, as you wish.

Gopal : Have a pleasant journey.

CS-610 : FOUNDATION COURSE IN ENGLISH FOR COMPUTING
JUNE 2003

Note : *There are six questions in this paper. Question number **1** is **compulsory** and carries 30 marks. Attempt any **three** from the rest.*

Q1. Read the passage given below and answer the questions which are based on it:

Robotics must be the most popular or well known application of artificial intelligence. It has been a major factor in factory automation. A loose definition of a robot is a type of automation that replaces human presence. But robot can be completely defined as a computer-controlled device that can physically manipulate its surroundings. There is a wide variety of robots of different sizes and shapes, each designed with a particular function in mind. Often these are functions that would be tedious or dangerous for humans to perform.

In factory automation, most robots handle specialised tasks such a cutting, drilling, painting or welding. Most Robots are designed to do a single function, following the same pattern of motion day after day. However some robots are programmed to perform a series of operations. They are equipped with sensors such as machine vision or tactile feedback, which enables them to rectify in case they miss the target as per the direction of the program. Machine vision helps the robot to take a snapshot of the object being worked on and execute a series of motions based on the object's position. In tactile sensing, a robot can feel a surface and take the necessary action based on the texture of the surface.

Robots are also proving to be excellent workmen in nuclear and chemical installations where human beings cannot operate safely.

(i) State whether the following statements are true or false. [5]

(a) Robots are best suited in nuclear and chemical installations.

(b) Robots are always massive in size.

(c) Untiring, performing duties flawlessly, programmable and uncomplaining are traits of robots.

(d) Robots are of immense value in factory automation.

(e) All robots can be programmed to do only one function at a time.

(a) True

(b) False

(c) True

(d) True

(e) False

(ii) What kinds of jobs are robots suited to do in today's world? [2]

In today's world robots are suited to do the jobs which are tedious or dangerous in nature for humans to perform. In factory automation most robots handle specialised tasks such as cutting, drilling or welding.

(iii) What do you understand by artificial intelligence? [2]

Artificial intelligence is the gift to robots, through which a series of functions are programmed in such a way that even when some problem arises, the robot can handle the problem by various alternative solutions. These alternative solutions are known as artificial intelligence.

(iv) Give a synonym each for the following words used in the passage:[3]
(a) tedious
(b) specialised
(c) target

(a) Slow, boring
(b) particularised
(c) object, aim

Q2. Fill in the blanks with the correct form of the Verb given in brackets: [6]

(a) It is a nuisance if the phone ______________ when we are watching an interesting programme on the television. (ring)
(b) I ___________ gas. There must be a leak. (smell)
(c) I ___________ the instructions but I don't understand them. (read)
(d) How tall _________________ you? (be)
(e) When I saw him he _____________ cards. (play)
(f) We ___________ breakfast early tomorrow. (have)

(a) rings
(b) am smelling
(c) have read
(d) are
(e) was playing
(f) will have

Q3. Do as directed: [5]

(a) His father is _____________ LDC in a government office. (Insert an article)

(b) They were here ______________ 6 o'clock. (Insert a preposition)

(c) "I am starting the day after tomorrow, mother," he said. (Change into reported speech)

(d) If I was offered a job ________. (Complete the sentence)

(e) I could not go to office. I was ill. (Combine the two sentences to make a complex sentence by using as adverbial clause of reason)

(a) an

(b) at

(c) He told her mother that he was starting the day after next day.

(d) I would have joined immediately.

(d) As I was ill, I could not go to office.

Q4. Rewrite the following in passive voice: [5]

(a) People expect better results soon.

(b) They were carrying the injured player off the field.

(c) Have you done my work?

(d) He has sent me a present.

(e) I shall sing a song at the concert.

(a) Better results are expected by people soon.

(b) The injured player was being carried by them off the field.

(c) Has my work been done by you?

(d) I have been sent a present by him.

(e) A song will be sung by me at the concert.

Q5. Write a composition in about 400 words on any one of the following: [12]

(a) E-mail - has changed the way we communicate

(b) Entertainment and Computers

(c) Terrorism - a curse

(d) An interesting Book

✓ **(a) E-mail .... has changed the way we communicate ⇒** It is true that E-mail has changed the way of communication. The basic meaning of E-mail is Electronic mail, which is communicated in the electronic mode with the help of a computer having modem and an internet connection to the other counterpart having the same facility. It is the fastest way of communication from one extreme end to the other of the World within a second at very cheap rates compared to other modes of communication. With the introduction of E-mail facility the role of postman has considerably reduced. The concept of writing letters and sending them through post is an old-age concept. The benefits of email are obvious...mostly it's quick. Also, many people feel that the rules for regular mail don't apply to email, making it less formal, which in turn makes email easier to compose and send. E-mail facility is being used in

government organisations, private firms, educational institutes and business world. Students widely use it when they want to correspond to the concerned university in which they study. They can solve their queries, check their results and get information about their studies right on time with the help of E-mail facilities. Through E-mail facility any person having his E-mail address can be easily contacted. This indicates that we can send and receive e-mails even when we are off-line. The mails collected through internet are kept in a folder created in your address. You can see the particulars as and when you desire. The Hotmail.com is the first E-mail facility provider.
From the above it is seen that the world has become a global village with the facility of E-mails.

✓ **(b) Entertainment and Computers** ⇒ Computers were initially invented and introduced in the markets mainly for scientific and arithmetic use. After few years, with its help the purpose of education, research and academic search was done with the help of computers. In general, people use computers because of its accurate working and skillful handling of work. Mistakes were avoided and large amount of work is done with less manpower. Computers not only consume less manpower, but also save money and provide more accuracy and perfection.
In the present scenario, computers are widely used for entertainment purposes especially by children. Movies, songs, photos are being downloaded from different web sites and can be seen on the computer itself. Slides, slideshows and computer games are being made on the computer itself. Mostly children are playing games on the computers to enhance their knowledge. With the help of software in graphics, the film industry have entered in a revolutionary age of drastic changes and producing excellent films. With the help of computer graphics only, films like Jurassic Park etc. have been developed and have gained an excellent response from the children. These graphics have eased out making animation films. Now a days, number of cartoon/animation films are being made on the computers without loosing much time with the help of animation softwares. These films can be seen on the Television also. For introducing stunts in the films, computer graphics are being used.
A film made in Hindi language can also be dubbed in any language with the help of computers. A black and white film can also be converted into coloured film with the help of computers in the field of entertainment. This was not imagined by anybody that the computer can change the entire world to this extent. Now a days, entertainment is the prime need of all of us and without it life is mute.

With the help of computers number of facilities are available on Internet like e-mail messages, e-cash, e-ticketing, booking of hotel accommodations and much more. Everybody having the required details can do all the above things from his residence and there is no need to run here and there. It is also possible that in the near future there will be no paper work in the offices. All the letters, drafts etc. shall be exchanged through internet without wasting time. This way the work will be done much faster.
From the above, it is seen that in the today's world computers are providing lot of entertainment to the people.

✓ **(c) Terrorism - a curse ⇒** At present, terrorism has become a dangerous problem for the entire world. When you see the newspaper or news in the Television, the most of the incidents are of accidents, murders and suicides. Not only this, you will also read about the terrorist activities going on in some or the other parts of the world. Especially, India has been facing this peril for the last many years. Terrorists have killed thousands of ignorant men, women and children in India, specially in Kashmir.
Unluckily, the world community has not paid any heed to India's agonies. The September 11 atrocities are commonly described as an event of historic significance. That is true, though not in scale; rather, in the direction the guns are pointing. For the first time in modern history, Europe and its offshoots are the targets, not the perpetrators, of horrifying crimes. Europeans have spent centuries slaughtering each other, but have not been attacked by their traditional victims. On 11th September, 2001, when the World Trade Centre Towers in New York and Pentagon were targetted, America for the first time felt the heat of terrorism. Thereafter only, he declared global war against terrorism and brought down the throne of Taliban Government in Afghanistan. The attack was mastermind by the activists in America and subsequently they targetted the Jammu and Kashmir Vidhan Sabha and Indian Parliament on 1st October, 2001 and 13th December, 2001 respectively. The terrorists are a group of people, whose basic object is to disturb the peace and harmony of the world. They are developed from the childhood and they are directed in such a way that they always believe in do and die. The terrorists are merciless and kill people at their own will and sometime even they use them as suicide bombers. They are always ready to die in order to kill maximum number of people. It is understood that they want to attack in bulk. They never bother and want to destroy human life.
Hence terrorism is a real curse and nobody has secure future of themselves and of their children. It is a fact that it will take years to build buildings and life but it will just take seconds to destroy them. Terrorism can only be curbed by combined efforts and not by an individual.

✓ **(d) An interesting Book** ⇒ The likings differ from man to man, some like playing, some like cooking, some like eating, some like wondering here and there but I like reading books the most. There are different kind of books like novels, stories, educational books etc.. I always like to read educational books. By reading books you can not only increase your knowledge but also can spend your time in an excellent manner. Whenever you get a book of your choice, then you can't imagine when the time has past. I read a story in the magazine 'Grah Shobha' which is very appealing to me. The story was of a retired policeman who was arrested and falsely charged with domestic violence by his then-girlfriend, who was a violent alcoholic, and who subsequently resiled her false charges. It was a very good story. From the story it was revealed that whenever a man or woman realises his mistake, he/she has to accept it. I also want to advise everyone of a most interesting book I read last year : The Myth of Male Power, by Warren Farrel, Ph.D. He was once a member of the National Organization of Women (NOW) board of directors, but he became disenchanted with the anti-male bias at now and resigned. One of the most interesting facts he presents in this book is that most statistics on domestic violence come from police reports. Most such reports are made by women against men. This makes sense, because few men who sustain physical attacks by their wives or girlfriends bother to call the cops. I know this is true, because I used to be a cop. On the other hand, I also know—again because I used to be a cop—that women do attack men frequently, and those cases which come to police attention are usually called in by neighbours, or by hospital emergency room personnel due to extensive injuries or the involvement of weapons.

In other words, hospital records reveal that an equal percentage of men are battered by female domestic partners as are women battered by male domestic partners.

Anyway, I highly recommend this book. It's very readable, and contains many other fascinating facts and statistics. Also intersting book can prove to be useful like a friend.

Q6. Write a dialogue in about 150 words on any one of the following topics: [10]

(a) Your teacher tries to convince you to spare some time regularly for physical exercise

Teacher : Krishna, please come here.

Krishna : Yes, Sir.

Teacher : What has happened to you? You are looking very serious and not taking any interest in physical exercise. Are you Ok.

Krishna : I am OK, Sir but I do not know what happened to me.

Teacher : Are you going to the Park nearby to your residence in the morning and do physical exercise every day?

Krishna : No. Not at all sir.

Teacher : Why are you not doing physical exercises? Do you know that physical exercises keep the body healthy and fresh and you might have seen number of people walking briskly in the morning and sometime on the green grass.

Krishna : As you know, sir, that my mother is not well these days and I am also preparing for giving the entrance examination for Chartered Accountant course. It is very difficult for me to spare any time for doing physical exercises.

Teacher : As you are aware that physical exercise in the morning keeps the body healthy, wealthy and wise. Also if you do regular exercise, it will make your brain sharper.

Krishna : Sir, what should I do ? Please advise me.

Teacher : You can go for a morning walk everyday. Morning walk is also a good exercise and you will definitely feel fresh throughout the day.

Krishna : Sir, my main problem is to get up early in the morning.

Teacher : Okay, don't worry. This is my responsibility to get you up in the morning.

Krishna : Thank you Sir. I will definitely join you from tomorrow.

(b) Your father asks you to spend less time watching T.V. You do not agree with him.

Father : Ramesh, what has happened to you, whenever I see you, you are found sitting in front of the TV and watching it continuously. As your exams are near, you should be devoting your time towards your studies to get a good position.

Myself : Oh, Daddy, I watch TV only whenever I have spare time after studying. Please let me watch.

Father : My son, try to understand. I am not your enemy. This will not only hamper your study schedule but also affect your health.

Myself : You are right Daddy but I am not watching the TV continuously. I generally watch 'Discovery Channel' which provides knowledgeable things.

Father : It is better for you, if you spend less time in watching TV and more in studies.

Myself : Oh, Daddy try to understand. I am much more serious about my studies. I can study for three to four hours continuously and after that I need some relaxation. After watching TV, I sit back to study and I can really study well.

Father : I am advising you, so that you should get good marks in your exams.

Myself : Daddy, don't worry. I will get good marks in this exam also.

(c) Your friend and you discuss your hobbies

Ram : Hello, Laxman everybody have some hobbies.
(My friend)

Myself : Yes, you are right. Hobbies can be compared with liking. As you are aware, that likings are different from man to man, someone likes eating, someone likes drinking, someone likes walking etc.

Ram : Well similar is the case of hobbies. They also differ from man to man.

Myself : What are your hobbies?

Ram : Well, my hobbies are reading, travelling and singing songs.

Myself : Your hobbies are interesting, I also like reading and singing songs.

Ram : What kind of books do you read?

Myself : I like reading spiritual books. What about you ?

Ram : I too like spiritual books. Oh no, our hobbies, in general, are the same. What about singing.

Myself : I like Hindi songs of Kishore Kumar and Lata Mangeshkar.

Ram : I also like them and I have already joined classes for the same.

Myself : Where have you joined the classes? Please let me know. I also want to join classes to learn western music.

Ram : I joined Bhartiya Vidya Bhawan.

Myself : I will also plan to join the same in the near future.
Please furnish the details of fees, timings and availability of seats etc.

Ram : OK, I will let you know soon.

Myself : Ok, bye bye, hope to meet you soon in Bhartiya Vidya Bhawan.

CS-610 : FOUNDATION COURSE IN ENGLISH FOR COMPUTING
DEC 2003

Note: *Attempt **all** the questions.*

Q1. Read the passage given below and answer the questions which are based on it:

Scientists in many parts of the world are now trying to reclaim the desert lands. In Iraq, with its two great rivers, everyone thinks immediately of irrigation. Actually irrigation is not a very important means of reclaiming desert lands. In the first place, only a small part of the world's desert land is near enough to large rivers for men to be able to use them, and in the second place, irrigation itself can be dangerous for the land, where a hot sun evaporates great quantities of water every day. In fact, irrigation may change fertile land to barren land, and indeed is doing so all the time. The reason for this is simple. All river water is slightly salty. If we spread river water over the land and allow it to evaporate, we spread salt over the land too. If we go on doing this, the land becomes so saline that it produces nothing but palm trees - and eventually not even palm trees grow there; the land has become a desert.

(i) Why does everyone think of using irrigation to reclaim desert land in Iraq? [2]

(ii) When does a piece of land become a desert? [2]

(iii) How can irrigation change fertile land into barren land? [2]

(iv) Choose from the passage the words which mean the same as the following: [6]

(a) salty

(b) land which produces vegetation

(c) to change liquid into vapour

(d) in the end

(e) to supply water to land

(f) to bring back into use

(i) Every one think of using irrigation to reclaim desert land in Iraq because of availability of two great rivers. Water of these rivers can be used for irrigation on the land in desert.

(ii) A piece of land becomes a desert when the hot sun evaporates great quantities of water every day and is no longer used for irrigation and it is waterless, plantless and lifeless.

(iii) Irrigation can change fertile land into barren land because of the salty water of river is brought to the desert areas. Due to hot sun, the water will evaporate and so the salt will spread over the land. Hence the land will become saline and nothing will be produced on it, so it will become barren land.

(iv) (a) salty - saline
(b) land which produces vegetation - fertile
(c) to change liquid into vapour - evaporate
(d) in the end - eventually
(e) to supply water to land - irrigation
(f) to bring back into use - reclaim

Q2. Do as directed: [8]

(i) Pick out the odd word.
(a) lock
(b) knock
(c) shut
(d) bolt
(ii) Give the opposite of lift.
(iii) Insert an article in the blank space:
He is late by ________ hour.
(iv) Complete the sentence by adding a suitable relative clause:
Did you collect the parcel _________?
(v) Fill the blank with an appropriate modal:
People with fair skin ________ be particularly careful when they go out in the sun.
(vi) Change into reported speech:
My father said, "Don't forget to go to the supermarket after work".
(vii) Correct the sentence:
She is understanding the lesson now.
(viii) Use an appropriate preposition:
She is very good __________ languages.

(i) Knock
(ii) drop
(iii) an
(iv) despatched by me.
(v) should
(vi) My father ordered me not to forget to go to the super market after work.
(vii) She understands the lesson.
(viii) at

Q3. Fill in the blanks with the correct form of the verb: [5]

(a) She ________ (go) for a walk every day.
(b) I _________ (prepare) for competitive exams.

(c) I __________ (work) in this office for five years.
(d) His mother _______ (arrive) from Mumbai yesterday.
(e) The thief _________ (escape) before the police came.
(a) goes
(b) am preparing
(c) have been working
(d) arrived
(e) had escaped

Q4. Change to passive voice: [5]
(a) I hope they will have completed all the work by tomorrow.
(b) People were using the tennis court so we couldn't play.
(c) They saw him climbing over the hill.
(d) People said he was jealous of her.
(e) We called the fire station when the fire broke out.
(a) It is hoped that all the work will have been completed by next day.
(b) The game could not be played by us because the tennis court was being used by the people.
(c) He was seen by them climbing over the hill.
(d) It was said by people that he was jealous of her.
(e) The fire-station was called by us when the fire broke out.

Q5. Write a composition in about 400 words on any one of the following topics: [10]
(a) Women cannot take up all kinds of jobs
(b) My favorite form of relaxation
(c) The value of Democracy

✓ **(a) Women cannot take up all kinds of jobs** ⇒ The above statement is applicatory in most of the cases, but in the present state of affairs, women are working with men and performing a variety of jobs. It is seen that the women have different temperament and life-style as compared to men. The society also looks at women with different angle and even the outlook differ for male and female members. In most of the families the work is divided in such a manner that the home is looked after by the women and the male members go out for work to earn money. A large number of jobs are being performed by women. Some of these are like working in banks, public sector undertakings, teaching in schools etc. and their works are being appreciated. They can work in the offices for limited hours and come back to home to perform traditional duties of a woman. It will always remain a question that when will our society consider a woman at par with the man. The women's ability has been better valued as a mother, sister, wife and friend. She has never been allowed to take a front position in the family.

A male is always at his liberty to perform any type of tasks assigned to him. He can perform night duties, he can drive auto-rikshaw, buses, trucks but this kind of jobs are generally avoided for women. But now a days women are performing night duties also. They have joined call centres where they are better performing night duties but they are limited in number. It is also seen that in some of the families young girls are not permitted by their families to go out for work. Few years back, the women were not allowed to join the film industry but in today's economy, many parents are encouraging their daughters to work in film-industry. Generally women are being allowed to take up some jobs in which they have to travel, perform night-duties, overtime etc.. Women performing night-duties and return home in the morning are not recognised by our society as good women. Most of these type of jobs require physical stamina and women are considered unfit for such jobs.

Keeping in view the above, women cannot take up all kind of jobs due to physical and social demands and pressure of society. The other reason is that home responsibilities are not being shared by male members and the same mostly rest with women. If women are permitted to work at their sweet will, they can perform better and break the barrier of progress, but this requires a favourable approach of society.

✓ **(b) My favorite form of relaxation** ⇒ Many years ago during a particularly unhappy and stressful period in my life, I felt that under the circumstances I was coping quite well. However, I soon realised that my daytime anxiety had a negative effect during the night. Although I slept fairly well, each morning when I awoke, I found that my hands were in tight fists.

It was quite obvious that the tension I was holding would be harmful, and I knew I had to find a way to relieve it while dealing with my difficult living conditions. Several friends suggested various methods such as hypnotism and counselling, but I felt I wanted to do something myself. I discovered the way quite by accident. While on a short holiday with some friends, we found that relaxation was part of the package. It was just for a short period each day.

At first I was quite unbelieving. I knew my mind was so active that I thought it would be impossible for me to relax. However, gradually it became a little easier and I began to enjoy each session more and more. The teacher explained that relaxation was just like any other physical skill - it improves with practice. Essentially it was the ability to 'let go'.

On my return from holiday, I felt calmer and I started to look for other sources of relaxation. I was surprised to find that there were a variety of techniques. One of the most popular techniques was to tighten each body part and then relax it. Personally this did not appeal as I found difficulty in releasing the tension when told to do so. I enjoyed a form of relaxation called 'autogenic'

whereby the teacher names each part in turn and then you repeat it mentally - such as "my right arm is heavy and relaxed". As long as the person giving the relaxation has a calm soothing voice, it is very effective.
The relaxations are usually done lying down and a warm blanket is essential. Sometimes it can help to place a cushion under the head or knees. Relaxation can also be practiced while sitting on a comfortable chair. This is good for asthmatics. I find that having to focus on the different parts of the body really does help to relax my mind, shutting out busy or anxious thoughts. However, it doesn't happen straight away. Patience and perserverance pay dividends.
My favourite form of relaxation is called yoga nidra, where an affirmation - a short positive statement - is used at the beginning and at the end of the practice. This works on the subconscious mind during the very relaxed state. Visualisation is also a very important aspect of this. Relaxation encourages the 'feel good factor'. Endorphins are released and the physical, emotional and mental benefits can help combat anxiety, insomnia and panic attacks. Relaxation cassettes are useful if a teacher is unavailable

✓ **(c) The value of Democracy ⇒** The word democracy literally means "rule by the people." It is derived from a Greek word coined from the words demos ("people") and kratos ("rule") in the middle of the 5th century BC to denote the political systems. It applies a system of selecting its leader by a proper system of franchise. Parliament elections are held in India at least once in five years. Anybody who is eighteen years of age is entitled to cast his vote. Now a days voting is being casted through an electronic voting machine, in which there is no need to take a ballot paper and then stamp. Just press the button against the symbol you like and your vote is casted. In India elections are held for Members of Parliament and Members of Lagislation Assembly. In India, to get an employment or passport, you need a police clearance but for contesting for MP or MLA there is no need of any clearance. As is seen from the present politics in India, the more the number of cases registered against you, more is the possibility of your winning the elections. Now a days, smugglers, drug peddlers, criminals were earlier financing and helping the politicians but now a days they have directly jumped into political life.
Democracy also means living life without any limitations, like a free bird. In today's life everybody wants to be free and live his life in his own style. Nobody wants any restrictions on him. The true idea of democracy and the true value of democracy is yet to be understood by us. We generally discuss about our rights. We have accepted the fact that we are leading a restriction less life. We all behave in our ways and enjoy our freedom. I think that while enjoying our freedom, we have forgotten the value of democracy. We all do not know the value of democracy. We do not think about our duties as much

as we all think about our rights. It is often said that something that becomes easily available loses its importance. We do not feel that we are free. It is just like the availability of air in atmosphere, we can feel the freedom but we are no longer conscious of it. We take it for granted. We have started misusing our precious democracy. There are number of examples, like we use laws to our benefits, buy everything with money power, we do not even think twice before damaging a public property. This itself shows that the value of democracy is lost. As you are aware, that everything that has a price also has a value. The freedom fighters have paid the price in getting democracy, so they know the value.

Q6. Write a dialogue in about 150 words on any *one* of the following topics: [10]

(a) Two passengers on a railway train

(b) A tells B that he had a strange dream

(c) Ashok asks Geeta for directions to the telephone exchange.

(a) Two passengers on a railway train

Passenger A - Excuse me, my seat number is 21. I think you are sitting on my seat, will you please check your seat number.

Passenger B - Oh sorry. It is your seat. My seat number is 22. Please come. I will take out my belongings from your seat.

Passenger A - No, no let them be there. I just have a very small bag, as I am getting down at Muradabad, just after three hours and I do not carry much luggage as I am going there to attend a marriage party and where are you going?

Passenger B - I am going to Rai Bareilly to my uncle's house who had a farmhouse there. I will stay there for at least a week. How much time will you spend in Murabadad?

Passenger A - Actually I have taken one week leave from my office. I have come to attend the marriage. After marriage I will decide where should I go.

Passenger B - Where are you working ?

Passenger A - I am working as a cashier in Bank of Baroda. Where are you working?

Passenger B - I am also working in Bank of Baroda. In which branch are you working?

Passenger A - I am working in Pahar Ganj branch and what about you?

Passenger B - I am working in a branch at Cannaught Place. Oh, we both are working in the same bank. I am very much glad to meet you. Why don't you come to Rai Bareilly after attending marriage? We both will enjoy there.

Passenger A - I am also glad to meet you. I will think over your proposal and in case it is possible I will definitely join you at Bareilly. Can you give me your address there?

Passenger B - Why not, please note down the address. Oh, your station has come.

Passenger A - Oh yes. I have to get down here. Any way see you. Bye bye.

Passenger B - Bye bye see you soon. Good night.

Passenger A - Good night.

(b) A tells B that he had a strange dream

A : Do you believe in dreams?

B : Yes, I believe to some extent. What happened, why are you asking such a silly question?

A : I am asking because I want to tell you about a strange dream that I had last night.

B : What did you dream ? Was it a good dream ?

A : It was not a good dream. I saw that an examiner was taking my exam in the Examination Hall and the questions mentioned in the paper were very simple and well known to me but I was not able to write.

B : What happened ? Why were you not able to write ?

A : The pen was in my hand and I was trying to write time and again but I could not remember a single word of what I had read. It was a painful experience to me. All the students were writing and I just sat there and cried.

B : Oh no. It was only a dream. Don't worry. I think that such kind of thing will never happen to you, as you are really preparing well. I also know that you are one of the brilliant students and always get first class, so I am sure, this time also you will get first class.

A : I hope so. Whenever I think of my dream I become afraid. Now I should prepare for my exams with more determination.

B : Because of this strange dream, you have become more active and I hope that this time you will not only score first class but also get distinction marks in all the subjects.

A : I will really try to get distinction marks.

B : You forget your strange dream and devote more time towards studies. This will definitely assist you to get distinction marks or even you can get top position also.

A : OK, thank you for advising me. Bye bye.

B : Bye bye, see you soon and all the best for your preparation and examination.

(c) Ashok asks Geeta for directions to the telephone exchange -

Ashok : Geeta can you help me.

Geeta : Why not.

Ashok : Geeta, today is the last date for depositing my telephone bill and for that I have to go to Telephone Exchange, where is the telephone exchange. I have not seen the new telephone exchange.

Please help me if you have any idea.

Gita : Oh sure, I have deposited number of bills of my telephone.

By the way, can I know the amount which you have to deposit.

Ashok : Why not, the amount of the bill is Rs. 2,400.00. Why are you asking this question ?

Gita : Actually, there are long queues for depositing the bills in cash. It is better if you make the payment by cheque.

Ashok : OK, where is the telephone exchange?

Gita : The new telephone exchange is near to the Aggarwal Sweet corner near vegetable market on Arya Smaj Road. Have you seen the shop.

Ashok : Yes, I have seen. The shop is at the extreme end of the Arya Smaj Road.

Gita : After reaching Aggarwal Sweet corner, you can ask anybody about the telephone exchange.

Ashok : OK, thank you very much for guiding me.

Gita : You are most welcome. Bye bye.

Ashok : Bye bye, see you.

CS-610 : FOUNDATION COURSE IN ENGLISH FOR COMPUTING
JUNE 2004

Note : *Attempt **all** the questions.*

Q1. Read the passage given below carefully and answer the questions which are based on it :

In their classification of the stages in the evolution of civilization, archaeologists use the names of the substances from which tools of different kinds are made. They use stone, bronze, iron, simply because these substances were used mainly for making of implements and weapons, and these objects, lost, broken, discarded or deliberately buried, have been able to resist, to some extent, the decay which occurs when most substances are exposed to oxidation. As well as the substances of which they are made, the way in which the tools themselves are made can characterise evolutionary changes, since an implement is always made by an implement, even if it is only one piece of Stone Used to chip or grind another piece of stone. So the Stone Age is subdivided into Paleolithic (Old stone), Mesolithic (Middle stone) and Neolithic (New stone) Ages.

Food production is often taken to mark the transition from savagery to barbarism. It is clear that planting trees and growing crops must have accomplished a great economic and social change for people who previously lived by hunting and by collecting and eating fruits, berries and herbs.

(i) Why do archaeologists use tools to classify different stages of human evolution ?

(ii) How does food production mark an evolutionary change ?

(iii) Stone Age is subdivided into how many stages? Name the stages.

(iv) Why were certain specific metals used? Discussed.

(v) Give a synonym for following words :

(a) resist

(b) decay

(i) Archaeologists use tools to classify different stages of human evolution to get atleast some idea of the stages for the names of the substances from which tools of different kinds are made.

(ii) Food production marks an evolutionary change as planting of trees and growing crops accomplishes a great economic and social change for people of different generations.

(iii) Stone Age is subdivided into three stages. These are :

(a) Paleolithic (old stone) Age
(b) Mesolithic (middle stone) Age
(c) Neolithic (new stone) Age.

(iv) Certain specific metals like stone, bronze, iron etc. were used mainly for making of implements and weapons.

(v) (a) resist - refuse
(b) decay - decline

Q2. Do as directed :

(i) __________ one eyed man murdered Jack.(Insert an article in the blank space)

(ii) I wanted to buy a bike but my parents wouldn't hear ________ it. (Fill in the blank with an appropriate preposition).

(iii) Correct the following sentences :

(a) Rama is resembling her sister.

(b) I work at the university for over ten years now.

(iv) Use 'little' or 'few' in the following sentences to fill the blank space:

(a) He has ______ little close friend and often feels lonely.

(b) We decided not to go on a trip as we had ____ money.

(v) Use appropriate modals in the blank spaces to complete the following sentences :

(a) Adam is late. He _____ have got struck in a traffic jam.

(b) Don't throw the picture away, give it to Aman. He ___ like it.

(vi) Change into reported speech :

Alok said, 'I grew these carrots myself.'

(vii) Complete the sentence :

If I knew her number _____________.

(i) a
(ii) of
(iii) (a) Rama resembles her sister
(b) I have been working at the university for over ten years now.
(iv) (a) a
(b) little
(v) (a) must
(b) shall
(vi) Alok said that he had grown those carrots himself.
(vii) I could have dialled

Q3. Use the correct form of verb :

(a) Rajan always ________ the truth (speak).

(b) I __________ already ________this film(see).

(c) She _______ on me last evening (call).

(d) Who _______ America ? (discover)
(e) She _______ since 2 o' clock (sleep)

(a) speaks (b) have, seen (c) called
(d) discovered (e) has been sleeping

Q4. Make sentences with the following phrasal verbs:
(a) put up
(b) lay down
(c) pass away
(d) make out
(e) break down

(a) Kindly put up a draft reply to this letter.
(b) He should not lay down his blame on you.
(c) My aunty passed away last week.
(d) I can make out that you are well.
(e) You should not break down if you fail in entrance test for doing Chartered Accountant course.

Q5. Write a composition on any one of the following topics in about 400 words : [10]
(a) Problems faced by old people
(b) The bravest person I know
(c) Beauty is only skin deep
(d) Life without computers

✓ **(a) Problems faced by old people ⇒** The most pitiable people in our country are the old people. It is seen that mostly they are neglected in the family. Nobody in the family takes good care of them. It is also seen that they are treated as an outcase in the parties. In the past, in India's joint family system, its tradition of respect for the old people, and its general structure of senior ownership of property provided people over sixty with an honorable place in society and in their families. But with a combination of industrial growth, urbanization, and Western influences, these systems are rapidly breaking down, leaving many of India's old people without forms of support. Many of these people, especially the poorer classes, have also retired from jobs that lacked retirement benefits, leaving them without either financial support or the extended family's protection.

It is also seen that there are some old-age homes where old people are thrown away by their own family members without any reason. Such people are continuing to live their life without any purpose. They live in their memories. They are not even able to criticise openly about their family members. This type of situation is generally find in some rich families. It is really surprising that some prosperous families also send away the aged people to old-age homes.

Old people suffer a variety of problems, ranging from boredom and a sense of abandonment and loneliness which can indirectly lead to illness and lack of health care, loss of working ability, sense of inferiority and generation gap. Hence the problems of the aged people are more than that of young generation. Their image do not present a healthy picture of our society. We cannot consider ourselves educated till the right of the old people is not well recognised by understanding them sympathetically, encourage them to make further contribution to the society, affirm their contribution, respect them and give them concern and care.

✓ **(b) The bravest person I know** ⇒ There are number of people in the world who have the speciality of different kind in their nature. Out of which some are greatly remembered and never forgotten. I would like to tell you about the brave person whom I met in my lift. The bravest person I know is my next door neighbour, a man who is almost 67 years old at present.

You will be surprised to think that why I am quoting the example of such an aged man. I have the answer to justify with an example. I know this man, Radhey Shyam for many years. He participated in the struggle of getting freedom to India and a number of times he went to Jail. He also told me number of stories about his fight for independence. I could never believe of his, running here and there with a lathi in such an old age. He also praised the courage and strength received by him from Gandhiji number of times. He is good in nature and helpful to everyone. A few months back he lost his younger son and now he is alone in the house. He was really shocked when his son died, but even at that time he showed great courage. He started teaching children free of charge. He had enough money to survive and he was not greedy, so he did not ask for money.

Last month, when he was sleeping in his bed room, four thieves somehow entered his house by breaking the grill. He woke up and the thieves tried to attack on him. He does not loose his tamper and take out his lathi that was there in his house as a memory of his past days. He attacked on them and kept shouting for help. The neighbours rushed to his house but found that the thieves were in the pool of blood. All of them were badly wounded. They were arrested. I was really surprised that how can a 67 years old man can have so much of courage for fighting with four thieves. When I asked him, he replied that the fight for independence is still not over. I was greatly impressed by his courage on that day, so I strongly admire him and I term him as 'The bravest person'.

✓ **(c) Beauty is only skin deep** ⇒ A balanced physical and emotional personality is a prerequisite to success. Until now, beauty and its pursuit has always been the domain of the fairer male/female. However, now, things have changed. Today, boys are also visiting all-male beauty parlors and gymnasiums with the same aim in mind. Actually speaking, beauty is only skin deep! Yes, beautiful and glowing skin is a reflection of good general health of your body. Hygiene and good habits keep illness away. If we imbibe and practice good habits, we are less likely to fall prey to diseases. Why not put it into practice from an early age and make it a habit. In another way beauty is something that appeals to us in some or the other way e.g. we love beautiful flowers, places and paintings. Beauty is an art and passion. But the most lasting beauty is the inner beauty. Thus the concept of beauty is to beautify things.

To look beautiful, now a days, even if teenagers do not have any skin-related problems, they still feel they don't look good. The sensitivity level in teenagers is high as they want to be accepted socially and by their friends. God has made this wonderful world and has blessed us with beauty around us. We often go to visit good places in search of beauty. I think that beauty is something to be felt. The beauty of a person appeals to us when the person is really beautiful from within. The real beauty does not come only by visiting beauty parlours and dressing up well, the real beauty is the sharing of love with others, understanding pain in the heart of our fellow-men and sharing the grief of someone who needs our support. The basic aspect of beauty is from human feelings and not the skin. But there are different ways of understanding beauty, some consider beauty as beautiful skin to be appealing, others consider the features and yet others consider the personality. Hence it would be very difficult to say, what is beauty and who is beautiful.

✓ **(d) Life without computers ⇒** For an increasingly large number of people in this country, especially students, using a computer has become an ordinary and regular part of life and learning. It is almost impossible for us to imagine life without computers, and it's even harder to imagine not having the electricity to use them. Computer has become one of the necessity in the present life. In all spheres, computers are being used and performing the task in a better and quick way. Computer not only increases the speed of work but also the efficiency. Accuracy in work can be attained with the help of computers. Now a days computers are available in each field e.g. banks, railway stations, airports, Government or private offices. Even computers are being used at shopping centres and cinema halls. The day-to-day work in schools and colleges are being done with the help of computers. Big companies are planning their businesses, preparing the estimate of cost-planning, profit and division of work load etc. on the computers itself. The research work and data collection, with great ease, are being done on computers. Now a days, computer is helpful even in simple work like preparation of daily accounts to complicated work like preparing estimates and reports for combining graphic and mathematical data, can be done by computers quickly.

The computer is being used by students for study and communication purposes.

The use of Internet has enabled the young and talented students to find their information from anywhere in the world within a second. The internet facility not only provides students the facility to communicate with people but also study many courses through it. It is a real blessing for the young students. The internet facility provides any type of help whether it is tourism, hotel reservation, ticket reservation, shopping etc. immediately. The use of graphics has enabled the fashion designers to have new design with great ease. The ATM facility is a new creation of computer technology. People can withdraw cash from ATM any time because it works on twenty four hours basis.

Keeping in mind the above in view, it can be said that we are totally dependent on computers for almost everything and we cannot do anything so easily without computers. Life without computer is like a man sitting in a remote area having no one around him. Computers also help us to keep in touch with almost every new development. Hence I would like to say that life without computers is not possible if a man wants to improve in life.

Q6.Write a conversation in about 150 words on any one of the following: [10]

(a) A tells B to come for a picnic but B prefers to watch a cricket match.

A : Hello, are you free today. If so, let us go out to see an English movie at Regal. We have not seen any English movie since long. Today I am free and I have made a programme to go with you for seeing the movie.

B. I am afraid. I will not be able to accompany you. I have postponed all my works and have adjusted some hours in order to watch a cricket match. Why don't you go with some other friends?

A. Oh, come on yar. You know that whenever we are free, we always go together. There is nothing in the cricket match. Also this time Sachin is not playing due to his sickness. You can ask people about the result of the match when we come after the movie or we can take radio for hearing the running commentary.

B. I think even you can do that. You can go and ask the story of the film from some of your friends who have seen the film, as most of the films are based on the same story. While in a match, we will observe the reality.

A. OK, OK don't give explanation and also don't try to convince me. If you do not want to accompany me, its alright. I will see the movie with some other friend.

B. It is better Bye. Have a nice time.

(b) You have to meet Ms. Bose, your boss's niece who is arriving from Calcutta, at the airport. Mr. Bose describes his niece so that you don't make a mistake.

Mr. Bose : Mr. Ramesh, where are you. I hope you are on the way to Airport to receive my niece at the Airport. She is arriving from Chennai tonight by Air India flight No. AI-112.

Mr. Ramesh : Yes, Sir. I am on the way to Airport and necessary arrangements have already been made. I have also postponed the meeting fixed with Secretary, Government of India for tomorrow.

Mr. Bose - Oh, thanks, Mr. Ramesh. Sorry for the inconvenience.

Mr. Ramesh : Not at all sir. It is my pleasure.

Mr. Bose : As you have not seen my niece. I would like to tell you about her so that there is no difficulty in identifying her. She is five feet four inches tall with wheatish skin and long hair. She usually wears glasses and she has the habit of wearing too many rings in her fingers. She has a nice personality and is wearing mini skirt.

Mr. Ramesh : Thanks. It will help me in locating her very easily otherwise I will display a playcard. Sir, I have drafted some agenda points to be discussed in the tomorrow's meeting and kept on your table. Please go through them.

Mr. Bose : OK, I will definitely see. Bye.

(c) You discuss the importance of computer education with your grandfather.

I : My dear respected grandfather, you are sitting here and I was searching for you in the garden. Please come with me, I have to show you something on the computer. I have made a fantastic design of a book.

Grandfather : Yes, I will definitely come and see what you have done. But remember that traditional art cannot be copied well by computers.

I : No, grandfather. It is not correct. If you come and see my version, you will believe that computers can work miracles. Not only the design of book, computer provides us with the huge variety of design with different dimensions.

Grandfather : I, agree. You will also agree with me that whatever you have made, it is with the help of some people who made the programme on computer.

I : Yes, you are right Grandfather, but it is my skill to sketch out the design from the programme available in the computer. It is also a fact that everyone cannot make excellent design on computers. I think that in order to understand what I say, you will have to sit with me for some hours on computer. Now a days, I am of the opinion that in today's life computer education plays a very vital role and it is very important to learn computer.

Grandfather : OK. If you insist, I will see and try to learn computer with you.

CS-610 : FOUNDATION COURSE IN ENGLISH FOR COMPUTING
DEC 2004

Note : *Attempt **all** the questions.*

Q1. Read the passage given below and answer the questions which are based on i .

Compact discs (CDs) have revolutionised the music industry with their surprisingly realistic sound.

The six-inch discs look like thin plastic sandwiches with aluminium in the centre . They have digitally recorded material that is read by laser beams, so the sound has none of the cracking of vinyl records. CDs are also virtually indestructible, and they are lighter and smaller hen the conventional records. Since their introduction, CDs have become more affordable and widely available. In fact, they are now sold in electronic and video stores that haven't formerly carried records or cassettes.

There has been a phenomenal growth in the sale of CDs. Sales climbed dramatically during the second half of the 1980s. In the 1990s, sales have been even greater. CDs have all but replaced records in stores, and in spite of their being less affordable than cassettes, continue to gain in popularity.

(i) What is the main appeal of CDs ?

(ii) With which word can you best replace the word revolutionised' 'as used in the first line ?

(iii) Write at least three advantages of CDs listed in the passage.

(iv) When were the sales more, in 1980s or in 1990s ?

(v) What dose the word 'phenomenal' as used in the passage, indicate ?

(vi) What is the main idea of this passage ? Explain in two or three sentences.

(i) The main appeal of CDs is their realistic sound.

(ii) The word 'revolutionised' can be replaced with overturned or inspired'.

(iii) The three advantages of CDs listed in the passage are :

(a) Realistic sound

(b) CDs are indestructible

(c) Lighter and smaller than the conventional records.

(d) Readily Widely available and affordable.

(iv) In 1990s sales were more.

(v) The word 'phenomenal' as used in the passage indicates that there has been a fantastic increase in the sale of CDs.

(vi) The main idea of this passage is that CDs are very useful. They occupy lesser space. They are lighter, smaller and indestructible. The audio recorded data gives realistic sound.

Q2. Do as directed :

(i) Fill in the blank with a suitable proposition. The fourth generation computers were first introduced _________ the late 1970s.

(ii) Correct the following sentence :

Have you packed all your baggages ?

(iii) To complete the sentence, fill in the blank with a suitable article :

He is __________ honourable man.

(iv) Fill in the blank with a suitable modal.

I wonder why Ram hasn't answered my letter ? He ______ be ill.

(v) Change into reported speech :

"You'd better were a coat. It's very cold ," he said.

(vi) Use the following words in one sentence each to bring out the difference in meaning :

(a) fair

(b) fare

(vii) Comlete the sentence by adding a suitable relative clause.

Please return the books ________________.

(viii) Give one word that has the same vowel sound as in 'hot'.

(ix) make a sentence using the phrasal verb 'give up'.

(i) in

(ii) Have you packed all your baggage ?

(iii) an

(iv) should

(v) He said that she should have better worn a coat because it was too cold

(vi) The fare to see the fair at Pragati Maidan worked out to Rs.100/-.

(vii) Please return the books as soon as you finish.

(viii) pot

(ix) In the second round, the challenger gave up.

Q3. Change the following sentences to passive voice :

(i) They threw away the old newspapers.

(ii) How does he operate the machine?

(iii) He gave me a book.

(iv) Inform the police.

(v) The engineers ware discussing the details of the project.

(i) The old newspapers were thrown away by them.

(ii) How is the machine operated by him?

(iii) A book was given to me by him.

(iv) Let the police be informed.

(v) The details of the project were being discussed by the engineers.

Q4. Fill in the blanks with the correct tense form of the verbs given in brackets:

(i) He _____________ (smoke) at least fifty cigarettes a day.

(ii) They_____________ (fly) kites last Sunday at this time.

(iii) He _____________ (write) a report when I_________(knock) at the door.

(iv) Renu ____________ (be) fond of dogs.

(i) smokes (ii) were flying

(iii) was writing, knocked (iv) is

Q5. Write a dialogue in about 150 words on any one of the following:

(i) You and your friend are planning to go on a trek to the mountains. Decide on the things you need to take along with you.

(1) A pair of lightweight hiking/trekking boots, suitable for walking over rough terrain, offer good ankle support and will be comfortable over long distances.

(2) Heavyweight gloves or mittens with a waterproof outer

(3) Down vest and/or jacket (optional)

(4) Fleece or wool trousers/pants

(5) Trekking/Hiking boots with spare laces

(6) Thick, warm wool hiking socks

(7) Footwear for around camp, e.g. running shoes and/or sandals

(8) Gaiters : These "alpine" gaiters are widely available. There are more expensive gaiters which cover the whole of the boot uppers, providing additional warmth and protection, and these are a sensible option for those trips which involve the negotiation of several days of snow-covered glaciers.

(9) Telescopic trekking/ski poles

(10) Sleeping bags and the rest mattresses.

(11) A wide-brimmed sunhat or headscarf should be used to keep the sun off your head.

(12) Water bottles.

(ii) You discuss the recent one-day cricket match between India and Pakistan with your friend.

Hello, Raju did you see the one day cricket match played between India and Pakistan.

Raju : Yes, I saw that match. India won the toss and selected to bat first and made a total of 275 runs for six wickets. Did you see the inning played by Sachin? He scored brilliant 85 runs. You see, no one can predict results in the game of cricket.

I know and India finally lost the match. The good innings played by Sachin and Ganguly were of no use. Pakistani players also played well. But I regret to see that when Imran was playing and missed the ball, the ball touched his leg portion and he should have been given LBW. An appeal made by Rahul was turned down. Basically he was out.

Raju : Yes, you are right. It is not possible to turn down the decision of umpire in the game. May be due to this Pakistan won the match. I think there may be some match fixing. It is a bad practice and defaming the name of cricket. What do you say?

I do not agree with you because they have considered the suggestion of third empire before giving the decision. What are you doing now? I am going to sleep. OK bye bye. See you soon.

(iii) You tell your friend the advantages of the course you have joined with IGNOU

Hai Ram where are you. I am searching for you to tell you that I have joined Bachelor of Computer Applications (BCA), three year degree course at Indira Gandhi National Open University , Maidan Garhi through correspondence. I have many advantages of learning this course from IGNOU. It allows students to study at a time, pace and place convenient to their needs. Learning can therefore be integrated into existing commitments whether they are professional, personal or domestic. Because of this, distance learning is an increasingly popular method of course delivery for busy professionals wishing to update their practice or continue their academic development. Students can also benefit from the trend within the University towards mixed mode delivery where students can choose a certain component of their course to be undertaken by distance learning. Although the student is studying at a distance from the University, the importance of supporting students through their programme or course of study is well recognised. The University has in place a wide range of support systems to help distance learning students at various stages of the learning process. This is accomplished in a variety of ways from the study centres. In many courses students also have the opportunity to network with other learners through a range of media options such as teleconferencing, videoconferencing, the internet (email) etc.

Q6. Write a composition in about 250 words on any one of the following:
(i) The merits and demerits of Internet

✓ **Demerits of Internet ⇒** There are still a lot of people out there who see the Internet as a promoter of immorality with all the pornographic materials. Let us ask ourselves. Is that all that there is in the Internet? I once asked a student from a rural area in my class if they had Internet connection in their house. The reply was his father would not allow due to the usual concern, you know what.

Besides the demerit of X rated material there are problems of hacking, using email / chat to kidnap / cheat a person on the other side has also be seen.

✓ **Merits of Internet** ⇒ The Internet offers various useful tools for communication, among which we might mention electronic mail, the World Wide Web, newsgroups, remote access, file transfer and text-based and voiced-based chat. The net has become the most important e-mail system in the world because it connects so many people worldwide, creating a productivity gain. Organizations use it to facilitate communication between employees and offices, and to communicate with customers and suppliers. Friends and family use e-mail in replacement to snail mail, due to its speed and flexibility.

Usenet Newsgroups or Forums are worldwide discussion groups in which people share information and ideas on defined topics of different ranges.

Telnet is yet another communication function of the Internet. It allows someone to be on one computer system while doing work on another.

Information retrieval is the second basic Internet function. Many use the Internet to locate and download some of the free, quality computer software that has been made available by developers on computers all over the world.

File transfer protocol (FTP) is used to access a remote computer and retrieve files from it. FTP is a quick and easy method if you know the remote computer site where the file is stored. Once a file has been located, FTP makes transfer of the file to your own computer very easy. There are hosts of directories that have been made accessible for FTP to search for files and businesses can use them to locate files they require for their operations.

Like FTP, Gophers are another information retrieval tools that can be used to access files. A gopher is a computer client tool that enables the user to locate information stored on Internet gopher servers through a series of easy-to-use, hierarchical menus. Most files and digital information that are accessible through FTP also are available through gophers. The Internet has thousands of gopher server sites throughout the world. What makes gopher sites easy to use is that each gopher site contains its own system of menus listing subject-matter topics, local files, and other relevant gopher sites.

There are also educational resources on the Internet. They are in various forms such as journals and database on various aspects of knowledge. For example there are sites where one can access online journals, or learn English. These sites are of tremendous help to those who are doing academic research. There are also special homepages on special topics or subjects of interest. At the moment, not many people use the Internet for this purpose. It is time we encourage our students to visit these educational sites, especially the English language ones and this will go a long way to improve their level of English.

Commerce on the Internet is already a reality. The communication facilities which are on offer have rapidly become integrated as core business tools. Thus most of the business functions are communicative in nature. The emphasis

to date has been on use of the Internet for communications with customers and other companies operating on collaborative ventures.
However, an increasing number are concentrating on transactions between businesses and on-line sales. The Internet Mall companies offer everything from books to flowers to travel. Trading partners can directly communicate with each other without passing through middlemen and inefficient multilayered procedures.
The Internet provides a public and universally available set of technologies for these purposes. Therefore, the Internet is rapidly becoming the technology of choice for electronic commerce because it offers businesses an even easier way to link with other businesses and individuals at a very low cost. Handling transactions electronically can reduce transaction costs and delivery time for some goods, especially those that are purely digital (such as software, text products, images, or videos
Marketing Communication is another business function of the Internet. As the term implies, marketing communication involves the use of communication media to market a product, goods and services. The nature of marketing communication at present is different from the mass communication paradigm of old. In the present era, marketing communication is more likely to involve expenditure on direct response marketing than involve the mass communication paradigm of old.
With the advent of the Internet, this traditional view of communication media has been altered. What we have now is the new many – to – many marketing communication model defining the web or Internet. This offers a radical departure from traditional marketing environments.
✓ **Concluding Remark** ⇒ The Internet is thus a boon for the Indian society since every activity or function of the society is covered. However, as it is at the moment, there are lots of benefits for businesses. It is therefore time we educate our society, especially the youngsters what to do on the net instead of denying them the opportunity to use it for fear of 'x' rated materials.
✓ **(ii) Clean surroundings help prevent diseases** ⇒ It is true that clean surroundings help prevent from diseases. Increasingly people are becoming aware of the lack of clean surroundings in cities and its health consequences. The poor in the slums especially, face piling of garbage, filthy and insufficient number of toilets, overflowing drains, stagnant pools and polluted drinking water, which spread disease and make their lives miserable. Not only this, now a days the whole of the environment is polluted by increase in the number of vehicles plying, factories and cutting of forest and atomic experimentation have polluted the environment badly and have disturbed the schedule of timely rain fall. However, it is not the poor alone who can solve these problems. Those living in better areas should realise that lack of cleanliness in one part of

the city, will affect the health of all. Due to various constraints, the public authorities are unable to adequately handle the huge problems of the cities and this has given rise to the unclean city. Life is becoming faster and faster and everybody wants a neat and clean surrounding. People wake up early in the morning and go to parks for want of neat and clean surroundings. They do yoga in the park for want of good health. We hardly get fresh air to breathe and pure water to drink, resulting in many diseases. Generally, the leaders organise simple garbage cleaning within the community, but for infrastructure issues like broken drain pipes, polluted drinking water and toilets they contact and co-ordinate with the municipal authorities. Continuous education in cleanliness and discussion with members, ongoing identification of local needs and daily co-ordination and pressuring of the municipal authorities are required to overcome the situation.

(iii) Different ways in which society can make life easier for the physically challenged

There are different ways in which society can make life easier for the physically challenged persons. Most disabled people feel that the disability itself, the pain, the need for compensatory devices and assistance can produce considerable inconvenience, but that very often these become minimal or are forgotten once the individual makes the transition to everyday life. But the discriminatory attitudes and thoughtless behaviours, these are what make life difficult, these are the sources of oppression. The architectural barriers; the pitying stares and frightened avoidance; the unaware assumptions that a disabled woman can't do the job, can't order for herself in a restaurant, can't find a mate or direct her own life, are all symptoms of the problem. The oppression is what's disabling about disability. However, it is also true that an individual's impairment do have a direct effect on his/her experience of being disabled, including the intensity of that experience, and it can be very helpful to unite with others with the same impairment. Indeed, for people with certain illnesses and conditions, including HIV/Aids, organising around those experiences has been crucial for obtaining better provision. It is equally true that the medical model of disability is still prevalent outside areas controlled or affected by the disability rights movement, making it a major factor within the social model of disability. And since every individual's needs are different, it is necessary to discuss the nature of their impairment in order to establish and meet those needs. The main assistance society can provide is to avoid discriminatory attitude towards them and provide them with the requisite alternative things according to their requirements. Also there are number of features available that provide physically challenged users with alternative methods to access.

CS-610 : FOUNDATION COURSE IN ENGLISH FOR COMPUTING
JUNE 2005

Note : *Attempt all* ***the*** *questions.*

Q1. Read the passage given below and answer the questions which are based on it. :

Global warming is a term used by scientists and environmentalists who see recent atmospheric temperature increases as the result of human industrial and agricultural activity and who believe that in the near future such increases could result in dangerous climatic changes. Since the end 19th century the average global atmospheric temperature has risen by about 1° Celsius, but until the 1960s, this rise was considered a natural fluctuation unrelated to human activity. However, many scientists and environmentalists now maintain that the atmosphere is indeed warming more rapidly than in the past, and will continue to do so, given the present circumstances, primarily because if increased amounts of carbon dioxide and other gases in the atmosphere as a result of the burning of fossil fuels – oil, coal, peat, and natural gas – and the loss of green plants and trees through deforestation. As further evidence, they point to the strong correlation throughout the earth's history between carbon dioxide concentrations and atmospheric temperature and to models of atmospheric processes that analyse past changes and predict future warming.

(i) Why are the scientists and environmentalists worried about the future? [1]

The scientists and environmentalists are worried about the future because of the continuing trend of global warming i.e. increase in average temperature on the earth.

(ii) Give two reasons for increased amounts of carbon dioxide in the atmosphere. [2]

The carbon di oxide has increased because of

A) Burning of fuels like coal, oil etc.

B) Cutting of trees i.e. Deforestation as trees help in reducing carbon di oxide.

(iii) Find out (from the passage) a word each having similar meaning as the following words : [1]

proof, quickly

Proof : evidence
Quickly : rapidly

(iv) Write a sentence using the word 'warm' in a sense other than the one in the passage. **[1]**
He was totally influenced by Ravi's warmth of love and care.

(v) How can the use of computers help in solving the problem of global warming ? **[1]**
Computer models help in analyzing and studying the atmospheric changes happened over the long past and predicting the future course of atmospheric changes.

(vi) Which of the following statements are *True* of *False* according to the passage ? **[4]**
For those that are true, write the corresponding sentences from the passage. For those that are false, write the corrected statements.
(a) Up until the 1960s, global warming was definitely due to natural factors.
(b) Global atmospheric temperature was less in the 19th century than in the 20th.
(c) Atmospheric temperature is independent of carbon monoxide concentrations.
(d) The above passage is merely factual, it neither expresses concern nor approval.
(a) True
(b) True
(c) False
(d) False
This passage shows approval of the fact that Global and concern wasming is happening.

2(a) Change the following sentences to passive voice : **[2]**
(i) Many countries do not play cricket.
Cricket is not played by many countries.

(ii) A small number of people are contesting the election this time.
This time the election is contested by a small number of people

(b) Fill in the blanks below with the correct tense forms of the verbs given in brackets : **[3]**

(i) I guess someone ______________ (come); I hear footsteps.
(ii) She _____________ (write) so much better now than she used to.
(iii) I ____________ (read) the instructions but I don't understand them.

(i) has come
(ii) writes
(iii) have read

Q3. In the following, do as directed :

(i) Correct the following sentences : [3]

(a) The cat fell in well.

The cat fell into the well.

(b) Time and money both are required to play polo.

Time and money Both are required to play polo.

(c) I am understanding the lesson now.

I understand the lesson now.

(ii) Complete the sentence with a suitable question tag : [1]
They haven't finished the job <u>have they</u> ?

(iii) Fill in the blank with a suitable article (a, an, the) : [1]
One of our neighbours is __a___ teacher.

(iv) Use the following words in one sentence each to bring out the difference in their meanings. You may change the form of words if required. [2]

(a) dose

Take two doses daily and get well.

(b) doze

He was dozing on duty.

(v) Complete the sentence by adding a suitable relative clause : [1]
Give me a book <u>which takes hours to be read</u> .

(vi) Make a sentence using the phrasal verb 'give' in' [1]

He gave in all the money he had.

(vii) Change into reported speech : [1]
"Can't you do it ?" he asked her.

He asked her if she could do that.

Q4. Write a paragraph in about 150 words on any *one* of the following. The topic sentence is given to you. Develop it keeping in mind unity, order and coherence. [5]

(i) Junk food is great, but then...

Junk food is great, but then obesity and heart problems and many other fatal diseases are free gifts. Pizzas, burgers, hot dogs, seem delicious and younger generation is living on them but everything delicious is not necessarily healthy. Junk food contains oil which is fatty. It leads to obesity. Junk food contains some kind of fats which don't get burnt even on working or exercising and they just stuck up below the skin. Junk food also provides a large no. Of hollow calories which just add to the calorie intake but don't raise our energy level. Junk food has come from other countries especially use and it is not and Indian concept. It is also causing maladjustment with India's hot climate and lifestyles. But a college canteen without burgers and hot dogs must be a joke. The younger generation loves junk food. But they must be keeping in mind the negatives associated with junk food and its bad effects on the health.

(ii) Suicidal tendencies are on the rise in the urban areas because...

Suicidal tendencies are on the rise in the urban areas because of various reasons. The first and foremost is changing lifestyles giving rise to depression. Depression comes from nowhere as every step is taken to compete. Life has become a race. Facilities and luxuries are alluring but income is not accompanying the dreams. Western culture is giving us a modern lifestyle with comfort of technology. Everyone loves comfort. So those alluring comfortable gadgets or a luxurious lifestyle or aspirations higher than the resources some people choose the wrong way leading to death in the form of suicide and those who try to chase their dreams honestly find life totally different from what has been written in the books. Other reason can be depression due to water tight surroundings life becomes hell when a family of 4-5 dwell in a single room. There is nothing such as clean water, regular electricity supply, green surroundings, and jam free roads. Suicidal tendencies are also increasing because of demoralizing family relationships. Life has become so fast that no one has time to sit and listen to the nears and dears. And moreover, life out side the home is so hasty and difficult because of increasing competition that generally that hasty life just to make survival possible takes its toll on family relations. Then there is no other way out.

(iii) More and more celebrities are endorsing products of all kids as it...

More and more, celebrities are endorsing products of all kinds as it is not important, where money is coming from as far as it is not illegal. And what's wrong in it? If one is getting rs. 50 crores for working 50 days in 5 years just for selling chocolates or shoes. There is nothing wrong in it? Celebrities are just adopting the same ideology. After all, money matters, and it is big also. The product endorsements deals have gone to crores of rupees. Mr. Bachchan is getting rs. 5 crores , Shahrukh khan is getting rs 3 crores and aamir khan has made his own class and claiming amount even higher. The other reason can be to encash one's popularity. If people love to see the celebrities on the T.V. Screens which they prove by increased sales celebrities are just encasing the sentiments. It adds to the popularity also. Mr. Amitabh bachchan is ruling every ad and every heart. So, selling chocolates, shoes, hair oil, home loans is not at all a bad thing to do.

Q5. Read the following passage and summarize it to one-third its length. [10]

Could this Product Kill Millions ?

ICI has announced the discovery of a new firefighting agent to add to their existing rage. Known as WATER (Wonderful And Total Extinguishing Resource), it augments existing agents such as dry powder and BCF (bromine – chlorine - fluorine) which have been in use from time immemorial. It is particularly suitable for dealing with fires in buildings, timber yards and warehouses. Though required in large quantities, it is fairly cheap to produce and it is intended that quantities of about a million gallons should be stored in urban areas and near other installations of high risk ready for immediate use. BCF and dry powder are usually stored under pressure, but WATER will be stored in open ponds or reservoirs and conveyed to the scene of the fire by hoses and portable pumps.

ICI's new proposals are already encountering strong opposition from safety and environmental groups. Professor Connie Barrinner has pointed out that, if anyone immersed his or her head in a bucket of WATER, it would prove fatal in as little as three minutes. Each of ICI's proposed reservoirs will contain enough WATER to fill 500,000 two – gallon buckets. Each bucket-full could be used 100 times so there is enough WATER in one reservoir to kill the entire population of the UK. Risks of this size, said Professor Barrinner, should not be allowed, whatever the gain. What use was a fire-fighting agent that could kill men as well as fire ?

A local authority spokesman said that he would strongly oppose planning permission for construction of a WATER reservoir in this area unless the most stringent precautions were followed. Open ponds were certainly

not acceptable. What would prevent people falling in them ? What would prevent the contents from leaking out ? At the very least the WATER would need to be contained in a steel pressure vessel surrounded by a leak-proof concrete wall.

A spokesman from the brigades said he did not see the need for the new agent. Dry powder and BCF could cope with most fires. The new agent would bring with it risks, particularly to firemen, greater than any possible gain. Did we know what would happen to this new medium when it was exposed in intense head ? It had been reported that WATER was a constituent of beer. Did this mean that the fumes would intoxicate firemen ?

The Friends of the World said that they had obtained a sample of WATER and found it caused clothes to shrink. If it did this to cotton, what would it do to men ?

ICI has discovered a fire fighting agent known as **WATER** (WONDERFUL AND TOTAL EXTINGUISHING RESOURCE) augmenting **BCF** (BROMINE-CHLORINE-FLUORINE). It is cheap and will be kept in open ponds and reservoirs but this idea is opposed strongly as people could fall into them and die or the leakage cannot be ruled out. One reservoir is sufficient enough to kill the whole countrymen of UK. It poses risk at intense heat as it is intoxicating in fumes as it is a constituent of beer. It also shrinks clothes so it must be harmful.

Q6. Write a composition in about 300 words on any *one* of the following topics : [10]

✓ **(i) The Problem of E-Waste ⇒** Information technology has surely changed the way we live. Life without computers is as horrible as death. Information technology has given us internet by which we can get into contact of a person who is beyond a continent within seconds through chatting tools. We can even see him/her through web cameras and there are many more positives added. But this electronic advancement has brought with it many things which are disturbing the society. On internet or on cell phones pornography is making the authorities sleepless. This garbage is spoiling our younger generation. It's another partner is cell phone. Cell phones with cameras are making life a hell. Everyday newspapers claim of having captured one's private moments on cameras in cell phones by someone else. DPS's MMS case, Mallika Sherawater, Priety Zinta and others so many famous persons doing something not to be viewed in public are examples of how this electronic advancement is taking its toll on lives of the people. Moreover, people are being cheated on the net. Cyber crime laws are being made but these laws are proving to be sting less. People with criminal mindset aren't leaving this space also. They are breaking the codes, entering into private spaces of the people on the net, doing illegal money transfers on the net, and selling things with fake names. Although internet has made life easier but it is also making life a hell as viruses are also being spread through e-mails corrupting the data on the host computer. This virus mania is costing the US economy billions of dollars annually. E-mails on one hand are quick but on the other hand these are also quick enough to defame one as mails or messages spoiling one's image can be spread in seconds. So all in all electronic advancement really can be a threat if not handled properly.

✓ **(ii) E-mail has definitely replaced the personal letter** ⇒ Gone are the days when one had to go to post office, purchase a bland letter, write it at home and again go to post office to post the letter. And it used to take four to five days to reach. Leave all this. Time has come to use e-mails i.e. electronic mails. Switch on the computer, get a net connection, make your e-mail I-d on the sites providing this facility, start typing the letter and as and when you finish writing it and send it, it reaches the proposed receiver. Isn't it great? E-mails have definitely replaced personal letter. Now one can get complete know-how of far away relatives in the other countries even, within minutes. Earlier it used to take more than a weak. And computer it has entered the villages even. Government is taking all steps to make Indian villages computer savvy. Moreover, e-mails have many more advantages over the letter written on the paper. With e-mails attachments can also be sent. These attachments can include a long file that has been created earlier or some images, or even moving pictures in multi media files. All this wasn't possible in earlier letters. And these mails are received even if the post offices are closed or post office employees are on strike. Even if the receiver's computer is off, mails will be received. Isn't it great? Now people are getting into this facility more and more. This e-mail facility is of much use in corporate world also. People are more prone to use e-mails as it is quick, and provides a lot of other tools which were not available earlier. An e-mail id is becoming similar to one's contact number. If one wants to contact the other guy and the contact is not happening leave the message on his e-mail id as it will be checked soon. On visiting cards e-mail address is getting as common as phone numbers.

✓ **(iii) I would change many things it I were the Prime Minister for *one month*** ⇒ Had I been the prime minister for a month as the functional head of the country I would primarily concentrate on fighting with the two major enemies of the country. One is internal and other is external. The internal enemy is in the form of corruption, dirty politics, poverty, unemployment and communism. I would try to clean up the administrative set up by taking more responsible and accountable persons into the cabinet. I would propose to make amendments in laws to make entry into politics a dignified affair. I would give prime importance to the development of our villages as many of our villages are yet to receive the electricity. And a farmer who produces food for whole nation needs special treatment financially and functionally. I would make policies and implement them strictly for the development of our villages and our farmers. I would ensure free education for children below fourteen years of age. As illiteracy is harming the country the most. I would make special authorities to trap hidden talent in the country. I would try to bring out innovative people hidden in remote areas as strongly believe India is an ocean of talent and I would trap its every single drop. I would give our youth their due. Young India is energetic, enthusiastic and has zeal to aspire and excel. I would make way for their dreams. Then comes the external enemy. Terrorism. It burns, it crushes, it breaks, when I see or hear the death of innocent people in the valley or in any other state for that matter. I would slap on the face of terrorism by giving a bit more power and freedom to our army. I would not tolerate any terrorist act. I would talk straight and cleat to any country, which is hurting our peace and harmony that our quietness doesn't mean our coward ness.

CS-610 : FOUNDATION COURSE IN ENGLISH FOR COMPUTING
DEC 2005

Note : *Attempt all **the** questions.*

1. Read the passage and answer the questions that follow :

As human civilizations have changed from agrarian to industrial economies, they have become increasingly dependent on fossil fuels (petroleum, coal and natural gas) and derived forms of energy (heat and electricity). Early agricultural societies depended entirely on the energy of sunlight to grow food, and the energy of physical labour for its cultivation and harvest. Domestic animals, introduced later, converted food energy into fats, fibres and proteins and provided greater physical strength to draw ploughs, pull carts and turn waterwheels. These early societies obviously did not require electricity or combustion engines to drive machines.

The invention of the electric motor and the internal combustion engine in the nineteenth century changed this orientation completely. Firstly, these machines were a startling boost to productivity. They enabled man to do far more work and to cultivate and harvest greater acreage. Secondly, machines replaced draft animals, with the result that modern agricultural operations became dependent on petroleum and electricity. An absence of either one would be disastrous to present food production throughout much of the world.

Essentially the same transition has occurred in energy requirements for industrial, transportation and domestic needs. One hundred years ago, electricity was a novelty, automobiles were a freakish invention and the diesel truck was unknown. Since then, all three have become essential. A modern city cannot exist without electricity and petroleum. Within another hundred years we will have to find alternatives for the latter, since the world's reserves will not last that long, but our need for electrical energy will continue to rise.

(From : *Ecology and the Quality of our Environment,* by Charles H. Southwick)

(i) Give a suitable title to the passage. **2**

Fuel and Energy – The Bloodline of Modern World

(ii) What is the collective name for energy sources such as petroleum and coal? **1**

The collective name for energy sources such as petroleum and coal is fossil fuels.

(iii) What two basic forms of energy were sufficient to support life in early agricultural societies? **2**

Early agricultural societies were mainly using sunlight and physical labour to support life.

(iv) What caused a change from the older system in the nineteenth century? Discuss briefly. **2**

Earlier manpower and sunlight was mainly used as energy, then came the animal's strength but 19th Century gave electricity and increased workability manifolds.

(v) What are the three essentials of modern life? Will they continue to exist in the future? Give a reason for your answer. **3**

Three essentials of modern life are electricity, modern automobiles and most capable means of transportation. No, they won't continue to exist in future as their demand is growing manifolds and their reserves are getting vanished with lightening speed.

2(a). Change the following sentences into the passive voice : **2**

(i) The police caught the culprits red-handed.

The culprits were caught red handed by the police.

(ii) The people beat up the terrorists with hockey sticks.

The terrorists are beaten up with hockey sticks by the people.

(b) Fill in the blanks in the following sentence with the correct tense form of the verbs given in brackets : **3**

(i) My mother________ (reach) home much before I left for college.

(ii) Usually she ______ (return) home by 4 o'clock.

(iii) I _______ (finish) my work so I can accompany you to the market.

(i) had reached

(ii) returns

(iii) have finished

3. In the following questions do as directed :

(a) Correct the following sentences : **3**

(i) These days travel is costing a lot of money.

(ii) You can't get good marks unless you don't work hard.

(iii) Neena and Reena both are doctors.

(i) These days travelling costs a lot of money.

(ii) You can't get good marks unless you work hard.

(iii) Both Neena and Reena are doctors.

(b) Complete the given sentence with a suitable tag question : 1

Sarita is very intelligent.

Sarita is very intelligent. **Isn't she** ?

(c) Fill in the blanks with suitable articles (a, an, the). 1

_________ woman in _________ wheel-chair is my aunt.

The, the

(d) Use the following words in one sentence each to bring out the difference in their meanings: 2

(i) advice

(ii) advise

He gave me so many advices but I followed none.

Ravi advised me to go through that route.

(e) Complete the following sentence by adding a suitable relative clause:1

She showed me the photograph of her friend.........

She showed me the photograph of her friend who fell from the roof. / to recognize me.

(f) Use the phrasal verb *take on* in your own sentence. 1

He took on the charge and came out victorious.

(g) Rewrite the following in reported speech :

She said, "Ravi, are you going to the market just now?" 1

She asked Ravi if he was going to the market just then.

4. Write a paragraph in about 150 words on any *one* of the following. The topic sentence is given to you. Develop it keeping in mind unity, order and coherence. 5

(i) Cyber crime is the dark side of computers.

Information technology book has made our life very comfortable and enjoyable. But cyber crimes are the darkest spots. Crime on net are accounting for thousands crores of Rupees. Fake companies selling goods, companies getting important details and then misusing them. Illegal fund transfers are few of the many forms of cyber crimes. It is really taking its toll. Security on net also costs hugely. Cyber laws are being made and special wing are assigned the duties to control the cyber crimes. The USA economy is spending so many crores of rupees to control it. But the solution lies in awareness and consciousness of the net savvy people. The main reason behind the increasing web cyber crimes is ignorance of the people. These crimes happen because net users generally tend to forget basic rules and precautions. So cyber crimes can be a hole in the shoe but a bit of alertness can punch these net criminals.

(ii) Population control is not the responsibility of the Government only. Just making laws in the Parliament or sanctioning the projects can make no country great. How can a bunch of leaders assumed to be able to control the population, if a billion people are not listening. Only Government must make efforts to control the population growth. It is merely a wrong perception. The people of the country contribute to the development of a country, so it is also a responsibility they have to share. It can't be thrown on the shoulders of the Government. People are the active factor in population growth, so their contribution to the population control must be immense. If Government is spending crores of Rupees to aware the people and still the people don't listen, it is their fault and assuming that the Government has a magic wand with which all can be done, it is an illusion that is hurting our economic development. Being educated, people must know that no country can be run without active participation of the people of the country. People must understand their responsibility and must be determined to control population.

(iii) We owe it to the future generations to protect the environment. Development in real sense means better life, not just economically but environmentally also. If we wish to live in a clean surrounding with greenery everywhere, we must also understand that our future generations for any reason will be no different. We can't live so selfishly that we just develop and eat up whole of their resources and give them a polluted environment. It is precious gift of nature which we have received from our ancestors and we owe it to our next generations. Further more, it is everyone's most essential need to have a cleaner environment. It is essential for the growth and development of the people and the country. As environment is not important just because it helps to develop economically as gives us the resources but it is important because all wealth is worthless without good health and health is directly associated with good environment. It must be genuinely accepted responsibility for the present generation to pass on cleaner environment to the next generation so that the circle of life moves on.

5. Read the passage and summarize it to one-third of its length. 10

The newspaper has always taken upon itself the role of mentor to its subscribers, but whereas the journal of the last generation took pride in its independence and the editorial chair was regarded as a pulpit from which serious views were uttered with a full sense of responsibility, the newspaper of today is a huge financial undertaking with the same outlook as any other limited company. The editorial staff have to run the concern so as to produce dividends for the shareholders; in other words, they have to make circulation, and if they do not they will soon be supplanted by those who can. Their independence therefore suffers a very grave limitation. It is further curtailed by the fact that a newspaper is as much an advertising medium as a vehicle for news. It is said that the price which the public pays for its newspapers covers no more than a third of the cost of production; the other two-thirds is accounted for by advertisement revenue. The need for maintaining the value of its advertising space in competition with its rivals makes it all the more important for a paper to raise its circulation to the utmost. Thus, as a matter of editorial policy, it becomes much less necessary to instruct readers of the latest move of the Government than to persuade them of the advantage they will secure if they become registered, insured subscribers and are fortunate enough to lose a relative in a railway accident.

After two generations of compulsory schooling, which has at least taught everyone to read, the business of forcing circulations up above the million mark has not been difficult once the method was discovered. The last Lord Northcliffe showed the way with the Daily mail in the nineties. He saw that there was a vast body of people who were not attracted by the newspaper that catered for the professional man and the club member, but who would be eager to buy a journal that would deal in an interesting and arresting fashion with the things that were really a part of their lives. He realized that unparalleled success awaited the newspaper that would reduce politics to a minimum, provide chatty articles on sport, hobbies, and everyday interests, substitute literary and theatrical gossip for serious criticism of books and the stage, and, above all, appeal to the special interests of women. Once this new policy had been put into practice, its commercial value was obvious enough. The other papers were bound to follow the lead of the Daily Mail sooner or later. The process was hastened by the influence of American journalistic methods. Since the War the transformation of penny journals has proceeded with sudden acceleration. In reaching out to an ever-wider public belonging to the lower cultural levels, most of them have

rapidly dropped in intellectual and literary quality until now they scarcely pretend to appeal to people of intelligence. They provide news and views, not for their own sake, but as a means of purveying a daily dose of entertainment that will save readers the trouble of turning to books. Last generation newspaper was a responsible voice of nation. But in modern world, newspaper is a corporate concern, striving hard to achieve bigger circulation, so as to ensure nice returns to investors. News and advertising now take almost equal spaces. Ads cover major part of costs with growing literacy means bigger circulation targets. This was initially done by associating newspaper with people's hobbies and interests. **Now newspaper is not as intensely news filled as they used to be**. Now they are entertaining and also acting as trend setters.

6. Write a composition in about 300 words on any one of the following topics : 10

(i) The negative impact of technology

Technology advancement precedes and follows the development of a country. It makes life very much easier. But in many instances it is also proving to be adversely affecting the life. One of the major drawback of technology is in the form of modern devastating weapons. Now the third world countries are having weapons that can dissolve the human existence on earth within seconds. Technology has given the men the power by which they can destroy even themselves. Technological advancement has also given us the power to consume the natural resources at a much faster rate than the rate of their replenishment and the sting can be felt as electricity, water, clean air, all are becoming more and more scarce. Nations are fighting for water. Technological advancement has also given the men the most powerful mechanical giants which be of **phenomenal** use by any yardsticks. But these machines are also emitting new forms of never heard poisonous gases causing deadly diseases. The most modern kinds of fuels are causing most modern diseases. Such as CNG in buses is liable for breathing problems. Technology has given us another headache in the form of most sophisticated crimes. Cyber crimes are recent addition which take much effort just to get caught. Life is becoming hell on the net. Another major setback of technology is the introduction of modern electronic gadgets which are surely meant to make life more pleasurable but when they are misused they create a serious headache. This can be substantiated by cellphone usage by youngsters. They are using it or perhaps mis-using it as can be read in the newspapers regularly. Technological advancement has also made men its slave. Now it is very difficult to pass a day without electricity or a phone. It is really affecting our lifestyles and making us lazier as everything is becoming more and more automatic. So all in all it can be said that although technology has made life much easier but it has also given some negative impact to mankind.

(ii) Noise Pollution

With growing economy and increasing pace of industrialization many negative impacts on the environment are visible. One of the major thing causing a great concern is noise pollution. Pollution of any kind is really harmful and noise pollution is not different. It is affecting the **lives** of the people to a great extent. **Alarming** levels of noises that can hurt or badly affect the hearing power are mainly due to non compliance to the necessary standards. As far as noise levels are concerned silent generator are to be put but no one takes care. The basic infrastructure of industries is not upto the mark for controlling **damaging** noise levels. The other reason for noise pollution is every growing flock of vehicles on the road. The horns of vehicles are really adding to the noise levels. A temporary but very serious rise in noise levels is caused on Diwali due to bursting of crackers. **Those week or two raise the noise level in the environment to an irritating extent**. One of the major factors causing noise pollution is programmes and functions, marriages, public meetings, functions are all arranged with number of loudspeakers. It really causes a great trouble. Noise pollution ives so many deadly diseases and it directly affects the hearing ability. Hearing impairment is not the only disease associated with noise pollution. It also makes a person irritated and affects the behaviour of a person upto a great extend. It also deeply affect the concentration level of a person. Poor concentration leads to inefficiency which in turn creates a lot of tension. In the modern world noise pollution is considerably eating up great resources, so the government is taking steps to control it. Government is making legislaions to check industrial activities and it is also applying measures to control noise pollution by vehicles or crackers, but the ultimate solution lies with the public which has to be more aware and concerned about the quality of environment. Without the active participation of the people all policies remain **strangles**.

(iii) The Uses and Abuses of Advertising

Advertisement is a tool that helps the corporate world to introduce themselves to their target people. Earlier the advertising was done through hoarding, banners, circulars etc. but with ever growing technologies options like TV, Radio and even Internet is taking a major attention. Advertising has really diversified in the modern era. But as every coin has two sides, advertisement too has many positive and negative aspects associated with it. Advertisement is useful in more than one way. First of all, it informs the consumers. It is advertisement that tells the consumer about a new product, its use and benefits and choices. Advertisement also pursue a consumer to buy a product that helps the company. Brand image creation is also done by advertising. Sometimes a consumer remembers a particular product by its advertisement. Advertising also encourages competition among the corporate world that does a lot of good for the consumer. But there is another side of the coin also. The advertisement also comes with a price tag. Crores of Rupees paid to Bachchans and Khans just to sell cold drinks or chocolates on T.V. and this cost leads to higher prices. The consumer suffers another problem with the advertising is that is creates unnecessary demand. It creates an artificial need in the mind of the consumer that it leads to unnecessary extravagant spending. Sometimes so much craze is created that people purchase it with borrowed money without even to use the product the second time. The major abuse of advertising is that most of the times it confuses and misleads the consumer. Throat cut competition pushes the companies to sell their products anyhow. They just don't follow any business ethics and just try to sell their product. Just to sell their products they just serve the half truths and mislead the consumer. Jut to outrun the competition they outrun the consumer. So the advertisements have some negative impact also which can be removed by the awareness and education of the consumer and an efficient administrative set up.

CS-610 : FOUNDATION COURSE IN ENGLISH FOR COMPUTING
JUNE 2006

Note : *Attempt all **the** questions.*

---

1. Read the passage and answer the questions that follow:

Computers are used in many seemingly different ways in modern life, to the point that they are frequently misnamed "electronic brains". However, all these different applications use the same basic principles, and all must be first analyzed as problems by a person before the compute can be used. For example, a computer may be used to perform routine work as a repetitive nature, such as maintaining the bank accounts of all of the customers of a bank.

Previously this job was done by manual labour. Bookkeepers were instructed about the rules to be followed for a typical account and then they applied them to each account. Now the computer can do this but the rules must first be established by a person. This is an example of the use of a computer to save human drudgery in processing repetitive information.

Computers are also used to control systems in environments where it is not feasible for humans to act, as, for example, in unmanned space flight. A computer may be organized to respond in predetermined ways to measurements made by on-board instruments such as radar and to signals sent from ground stations. It may also compute the position and the velocity of the spacecraft in order to find out where the craft is heading in relation to the desired destination. Using the information available, the computer can send signals to the spacecraft control systems to keep the craft on the desired course and to perform the planned manoeuvres. However, again notice that all of the operations had to be planned ahead of time by people. A person had to think out the response to each combination of circumstances and to organize the computer to produce those responses. Thus a person might have decided that the braking rockets should be fired with a thrust proportional to the velocity and the inverse of the distance to the target. When the computer is properly prepared, it can control the braking rockets, but the decision about how they are fired is made by a person when he writes the program.

The third major area of computer application is to assist people in solving problems that are beyond human capabilities. For example, a com-

puter can be used to perform long sequences of computations that could never be performed by people because of human proneness to error and slow speed. Such situations commonly arise in mathematics or engineering when computations can only be performed. Manual calculation of the stresses in a modern airplane wing, for example, would be out of the question. Although the designer of the plane makes the basic decisions about the style of the wing and how the stresses are to be analyzed, the computer makes it possible to perform the analysis in a practical length of time.

(i) Why does the writer think that the computer has been wrongly names as 'electronic brains'? 2

The writer thinks that the computer has been wrongly named as 'electronic brain' because it seems that it is doing many diversified activities but their lies same basic **principal** behind its every performance and its every activity is anyhow supported by human brain.

(ii) List the three major areas of computer application. 3

The three major areas of computer application are :

(a) To maintain and operate bank accounts

(b) To run and manage space crafts for space explorations in which human beings cannot partake.

(c) To calculate and perform the calculations beyond human capabilities.

(iii) In what ways has the computer saved man from drudgery/manual labour? 2

Computer has saved man from drudgery as it has made many cumbersome activities very easy e.g. it maintains so many bank accounts which would otherwise include manual entries in bulky registers **taking toll** on manpower. It also performs horrible calculations which would otherwise require many geniuses working for months

(iv) Find out words from the passage which mean he same as the following: 3

(1) Work in which you use your physical strength rather that your mind.

(2) An action planned beforehand.

(3) Things happening in a fixed order.

1. Drudgery
2. Predetermined
3. Sequentially

2 (a). Change the voice of the following sentences : 2

(i) The cheque issued by you has been refused by the bank.

(ii) Heat turns milk sour.

(i) The bank has refused the cheque which you issued.

(ii) The milk is turned sour by heat.

(b) Fill in the blanks in the following sentences with the correct form of the tense of the very given in brackets. 3

(i) Water________(boil) at 100 Degree C.

(ii) Have you_______(see) my book?

(iii) You______(drive) very fast.

(i) boils

(ii) seen

(iii) are driving

3. Do as directed :

(a) Correct the following sentences: 3

(i) I am understanding the lesson now.

(ii) All qualities and kinds of material is available in this Mail.

(iii) The house was shook by the explosion.

(i) I understand the lesson now.

(ii) The material of every kind and quality is available in this Mall.

(iii) The house was shaken by the explosion

(b) I am right. (Use a tag question). 1

I am right. Am I not ?

(c) He is_____able student but not_________ablest (Use proper article).1

He is <u>an</u> able student but not <u>the</u> ablest

(d) Abstinence________smoking will do you good. (Use correct preposition). 1

Abstinence <u>from</u> smoking will do you good.

(e) Use these words in your own sentences to bring out their different meanings: 2

desert; dessert

Desert – Oasis in the desert gave us hope to live.

Dessert – Trying different desserts is my obsession.

(f) He built a house. He built it at a great cost. (Combine the two

sentences into one). 1

He built a house at a great cost.

(g) "The earth is round," Said the teacher (Change into indirect speech).1

The teacher said that the earth is round.

4. Write a composition in about 300 words on any one of the following. The topic sentence is given to you. Develop it keeping in mind unity, order and coherence. 15

(i) How computers have changed your life.

Using a computer has become an ordinary and regular part of life and learning. It is almost impossible for us to imagine life without computers. Computer not only increases the speed of work but also the efficiency. Accuracy in work can be attained with the help of computers. Now a days computers are available in each field e.g. banks, railway stations, airports, Government or private offices. Even computers are being used at shopping centres and cinema halls. The day-to-day work in schools and colleges are being done with the help of computers. Big companies are planning their businesses, preparing the estimate of cost-planning, profit and division of work load etc. on the computers itself. The research work and data collection, with great ease, are being done on computers. Now a days, computer is helpful even in simple work like preparation of daily accounts to complicated work like preparing estimates and reports for combining graphic and mathematical data, can be done by computers quickly. The use of Internet has enabled the young and talented students to find their information from anywhere in the world within a second. The use of graphics has enabled the fashion designers to have new design with great ease. The ATM facility is a new creation of computer technology. People can withdraw cash from ATM any time because it works on twenty four hours basis. In the present scenario, computers are also used for entertainment purposes especially by children. Movies, songs, photos are being downloaded from different web sites and can be seen on the computer itself. Slides, slideshows and computer games are being made on the computer itself. With the help of software in graphics, the film industry have entered in a revolutionary age of drastic changes and producing excellent films.

Keeping all above uses of computers, it can be easily said that the computers have changed the lift of mankind. Now life without computers seems life in a remote area without any connection with outside world.

(ii) Distance education helps education reach all the corners and all the sections of people.

Distance Learning is an emerging industry that utilises technology to provide and administer higher education and corporate training. Its rapid growth is propelled by the space sector, Internet and the enormous opportunity embedded in global education. The main advantage of distance learning is that it allows students to study at a time, pace and place convenient to their needs. Learning can therefore be integrated into existing commitments whether they be professional, personal or domestic. Because of this, distance learning is an increasingly popular method of course delivery for busy professionals wishing to update their practice or continue their academic development. Students can also benefit from the trend within the University towards mixed mode delivery where students can choose a certain component of their course to be undertaken by distance learning. For the working class, many universities have started such courses long back, such type of learning is called distance learning. Assignments are sent by post, one can attempt them and send back for evaluation and correction. Tests and examinations are held regularly and promotion is gathered for next higher standard. Degree is also awarded. This type of study does not affect your service and a lot of time and money is saved. These universities have opened their study centers in all the major cities where the classes are conducted mainly on holidays. Important information is being provided at the centers. A very good knowledge is imparted by these institutions. The admission criteria of these universities is transparent and very simple. An over age person get an opportunity to enhance his skills by taking admission. Students have the option to study anywhere they like and study at their own sweet will. Students are also given sufficient time to finish their courses. For a graduate level course, the student can finish his programme between 3 to 8 years and can be registered again after 8 years if he likes to continue. Another advantage is that a very large number of students can be enrolled by a single university. The overall cost factor for the study including classes being organised at different institutions is also less, as compared with that of a full time course from a regular university. The study materials are delivered by registered post at the doorstep of the students. The Distance Learning India 2003 international conference provided an integrative model to enhance the learning environment through technology and provide a framework for redesigning instructional processes to achieve highly efficient and effective learning environments that supersede the geographic distance barrier.

The approaching reality of distance learning experiences, computer-centric school education, instant and enterprise-wide corporate training, and so on has made distance learning a crucial topic. The interest surrounding distance learning is created by the space / satellite segment, and the Internet's ability to rapidly deliver vast amounts of educational content.

The one-day international conference with the theme "Distance Learning - The New Frontiers" has created a forum for the distance learning sector to upgrade the expertise, technology and services to concerned users, authorities and corporate organisations.

(iii) Only the rich people have benefited from an open and liberalized economy.

While framing the constitution of India the leadership chose for the country the socialistic pattern of economy. The objective was to develop a mixed economy with the public sector playing the role of a catalyst in the growth process. With a view to ensure that the development process treads the desired path envisaged in the five-year plans, a regulatory framework was evolved. The objective was to attain self-sufficiency and to restrict foreign investment except for certain priority sector areas. The industrial policy announced by the Government of India on 24th July, 1991 proposed to remove the administrative and legal controls to allow industry to achieve higher levels of growth and to make it competitive in the international markets. The policy aims at substantially reducing the number of industries requiring compulsory licensing, promotion of foreign investment in India, automatic approval of foreign technology agreements, public sector reforms and to liberalise the Monopolies and Restrictive Trade Practices Act. While retaining control over key industries, private sector has been granted entrepreneurial freedom. **However, there are aspects which are for serious concern**. The liberalization has also encouraged the production of comforts and luxuries trapping the poor masses in the cobweb of consumerism. Demonstration effect has multiplied and the ever-rising demand for comforts and other luxuries has distorted the pattern of investment. The production of wage goods and goods necessary for social welfare has suffered for want of resources and consequently their storage has caused misery among the poor. Hundreds of small-scale units have closed down because liberalised imports killed the market for their products.

The liberalization has seemed to favour large industrial houses having big assets base. Opening up of few streams for private sector and removing restrictions on production allowed big fishes eating up the smaller ones. Relieving import quotas allowed just big companies to get sophisticated plants. Economic reforms were hit accompanied by financial and institutional reforms leaving small sector untouched. It seems substantially that liberalization in India favoured rich people and big industrial houses greatly.

5. Read the passage and summarize it in about 150 words. 10

Once again the Supreme Court seems to have done the job that the Parliament and the executive has long dithered over. In demanding that the central and state governments speed up the process of making the registration of marriages compulsory for all communities, the SC has understood the regency of this simple procedure that can help check the gross violation of women's rights in the country. Proof of marriage may not be a panacea, but it can go a long way towards controlling persistent social diseases like child marriage, bigamy and trafficking of women. It is actually baffling as to why the Centre has repeatedly rejected the NHRC's proposal for such a rule – in 1994, 1996 and 2000 – and allowed the situation to drift unchecked.

A large number of marriages in India take place in violation of existing provisions of the law. Despite the Child Marriage Restraint Act, which penalises under-age marriage, social sanction for this Act persists, mainly in states like Rajasthan and U.P., and ceremonies are performed openly and in large numbers. In the case of bigamy and trafficking, it often gets difficult for the complainant wife to prove her marital status in the absence of a proof of marriage. And this lacuna is also widely misused to deny marriage and thus, escape from paying maintenance or to prevent women from inheriting their husband's property. Gender parity is still a distant goal in this country. But steps like registering marriages will go some way in empowering women and helping them assert their rights.

In the case of marriage registration, unlike others where the spectre of the uniform civil code hangs ominously, the government has no cause to be worked about objections from the minority communities. In any case, the personal laws of the Christian and Parsi communities make registration of marriage mandatory while under Muslim law, the terms of marriage are recorded in the nikahnamma, a contract, which is handed over to the couple. What is really needed is to insert a provision in the Hindu Marriage Act to make registration mandatory. Four state governments – Maharashtra, Gujarat, Karnataka and Himachal Pradesh – have already gone ahead with this legislation. It is now up to the Centre to make this a uniform rule.

Supreme court, understanding the importance of making the registration of marriage compulsory for all communities in enhancing the status of women and stopping women's rights violation, has decided to do something substantial. Compulsion of registration of marriage can check child marriage bigamy and trafficking of women.

Although child marriage restraint act is there to stop child marriage but it is violated freely in UP and Rajasthan. In absence of marriage certificate, complainant wife suffers and leave aside the compensation of maintenance.

Leaving aside the objections or different rules under different communities like Christians, Parsis or Hindus, Govt must amend Hindu marriage act to make registration mandatory as it is in Maharashtra, Gujrat, Karnatka and H.P.

CS-610 : FOUNDATION COURSE IN ENGLISH FOR COMPUTING
December, 2006

Note : Attempt **all** the questions.

Q1. Read he passage given below and answer the questions that follow:

Sometimes solution to large problems can be fairly simple. Take the energy problem. Solution focus on redesigning the automobile, boosting the use of nuclear and other clean energy and so on. But we could make a simpler start, says Matt Prescott, a British environmental scientist. He wants a complete ban on the traditional light bulb. The cheapest way for developing counties to make optimum use of limited energy supplies, and for developed countries to achieve cuts in their carbon dioxide emission, says Prescott, is to augment energy efficiency. As a first step, he suggests making light bulbs –a major source of waste in energy consumption –museum pieces. This could even encourage people to 'aim higher' in increasing efficiency in everything from hot water system to home insulation, thereby cutting Green House Gas (GHG) emissions.

After all, it is domestic energy consumption that causes more than 25 percent of the global GHG emission of carbon, sulphur and nitrogen dioxide. Recent research indicates that the wider use of 'green lighting' can cut this dramatically. Compact fluorescent light bulbs, for instance, use only about a quarter of the energy of incandescent bulbs to produce the same number or more lumens. That they also last about ten times longer than regular bulbs is a bonus. Compact fluorescent may be more expensive initially, but the long-term savings would surely offset this. Light emitting diodes (LEDs) also offer an excellent to the light bulb.

It makes sense in energy-starved countries like India to have regulated energy-efficiency campaigns that could reduce waste and pollution, and stimulate innovation. Let's start with light. The public should be made aware of concepts like 'task lighting' : concentrating light only where it's needed. This avoids waste of energy and since task lighting uses lower watt bulbs, you don't annoy others in the area either with an intrusively bright light. The government could kick off the process by providing tax incentives to manufacturers to market more efficient fluorescent bulbs.

(i) What does the writer mean when he says that traditional light bulbs should be made 'museum pieces'? *2*

Ans. Traditional light bulbs should be made "museum pieces" means complete bar or avoid to lit these bulbs i.e.. not found in house.

(ii) List three ways to conserve energy as suggested by the writer. *3*

Ans. The three ways to conserve energy are as under:

– use of CFL bulbs

– use of light emitting diodes (LEDS) bulbs.

– Concentrating light only where it needed

(iii) Give two reasons why compact fluorescent light bulbs are better. *2*

Ans. CFL bulbs are better because

– it consumes a quarter of the energy of incandescent bulbs

– it lasts about ten times longer than regular bulbs.

(iv) What does 'task lighting' mean? What are its advantage? *1+2*

Ans. "Task lighting" means concentrating light only where it is needed. The advantages are :

– avoids wastage of energy

– uses lower wattage bulbs

Q2(a). Change the following sentences into the passive voice : *2*

(i) The President declared the exhibition open.

Ans. The exhibition declared open by the President.

(ii) My mother gave me a book on my birthday.

Ans.A book was given to me by my mother on my birthday.

(b) Fill in the blanks in the following sentences with the correct tense forms of the verbs given in brackets. *3*

(i) She ——(go) to work every day. But she ——(not go) today.

Ans. She **goes** (go) to work every day. But she **did not go** (not go) today.

(ii) He jumped off the train while it———(move).

Ans. He jumped off the train while it **was moving** (move).

Q3. Do as directed :

(a) Correct the following sentences :

(i) This novel is too interesting. *1*

Ans. This novel is very interesting

(ii) She hanged the picture on the wall. *1*

Ans. She hung the picture on the wall.

(b) Add a suitable tag-question to the following sentence : *1*
You have paid him fully———.

Ans. You have paid him fully **Haven't you?**

(c) Write a sentence using the phrasal verb 'look after'. *1*

Ans. Dr. Dinesh Verma looks after his patients

(d) Rewrite the following in indirect speech : *1*
She said, "Father, I have got a job."

Ans. She told her father that she had got a job.

Q4. Write a paragraph in about 150 words on any one of the following : *5*

(i) Mobile phones can be a source of great nuisance.

Ans. In the middle of a meeting, an executive answers his mobile phone. In a busy office there is a blast of annoying, impossible-to-ignore ringtones. An employee chats on his mobile with his child about school, while another discusses dinner plans with her boyfriend. Mobiles are becoming an increasing problem in the workplace. Mobile phones are very disruptive to the traditional workplace.

Is continuous innovation too much of a good thing? So much so that it turns not-so-good? In the fast-changing world of mobile phone technology, operators and service providers have to constantly grapple with breakneck changes, enough to confuse themselves in their race to please consumers. Innovations in technology would continue to pose the challenges for society. While it helps to improve the day-to-day functioning, operators would need to strike a balance when social networking goes mobile. Mobile phone helps commercial enterprises, media owners, housewife, children the whole nation to reach and discuss their problem. It also provides new revenues to the government. Thus it is difficult to say weather mobile is blessing or curse.

(ii) Advantages and disadvantage of email

Ans. Advantage of Email are : E-mail stands for electronic mail, which is communicated in the electronic mode with the help of a computer having mode m an internet connection to the other counterpart having the same facility. It is the fastest way to communication from one extreme end to the other of the world within a second at very cheap rates.

The concept of writing letters and sending them through post has considerably reduced. Students widely use it when they want to correspond to the university etc.. They can solve their queries, check their result and get information about their studies with the help of E-mail.

Disadvantage of E-mail are : Though E-mail has many benefits it cannot be spare with its disadvantage. In rural areas and small town due to lack of power and electricity E-mail facility cannot be availed. But the dangerous disadvantage are Terrorist activity, criminal and fraud person uses it world wide and create violence and havoc. Besides the unwanted mail send by unauthorized person create problems and also computer virus may be received through E-mail which destroy our systems.

Conclusion : Ultimately, we can say it is a boon in our modern time. Youth and professionals cannot live without E-mail.

(iii) Computer games.

Ans. One of the things that "Fantasy Writer" is about the importance of attempting to understand the pleasure others find. As you are aware that there was a time when children are playing video games with a pretty lonely experience in the semi dark room hunched over the computer screen. They are simply playing the games and they do not know the practical fantasy world of the game designer's making. Sometimes they assess themselves as hero in some puzzle-solving and sometimes painful, existence of their ordinary lives. But now all that is changing. Computer applications are not only used for games but also designing cars, trains, aeroplanes and even medical diagnosis of patients. The computers available in the market at present are equipped with the most modern appliances and well versed with applications like E-mail, E-com, internet surfing, multimedia, voice mail, business applications, CAD, CA, entertainment and web cameras. For video games there are number of web sites from where games can be down loaded. An Internet connection and a paid membership to the game's Web sites allow the subscribers to play twenty four hours a day. After installing the games on the computer, the player only needs to create a character to represent himself before entering this new game world.

The other world of fantasy with the computer is the Robots. They are computerized machines equipped with remote sensing devices and can respond according to their surroundings. Robots are generally used for the risky or repetitive works. The another world of fantasy with the computer is of animation and multimedia. The animation has created his own world of fantasy. Many of the stories and fantasy tales had been developed and made out of the creative thinking. Everyone has its own fantasy world in their dream and this dream comes true with computer by animation. A large number of computer games have been Internet and web based games are created which can be played any time at two ends of the world without knowing each other.

Q5(a). Fill in the blanks with suitable articles (a, an or the), wherever necessary : *3*

(i) —— girl in blue is my sister.

Ans. <u>**The**</u> girl in blue is my sister.

(ii) He is —— university employee.

Ans. He is <u>**a**</u> university employee.

(iii) It will be —— honour to meet her.

Ans. It will be <u>**an**</u> honour to meet her.

(b) Use the following words in one sentence each to bring out the difference in their meaning : *2*

(i) except

Ans. All students have passed except Ravi.

(ii) accept

Ans. Vicky accepted the offer of the company.

Q6. Write an essay of about 300 words on any one of the following topics *10*

(i) My Vision of India in 2020

Ans. India is a developing country. After 60 years of independence, we are still lacking in various fields of development. My vision about India in 2020 is very clear from infrastructure to agriculture to service sector and industry, to educative and health to eradication of poverty.

Agriculture : My vision about agriculture product is as much as that no Indian will sleep without having food in three times a day. This time about 24% of the population is living below the poverty line. In 2020, I hope it will be about 1% or nil. To achieve the target we all Indians have to do their best support to our farmers. Scientists need to provide hybrid seed fertilizers and such a production technology. So that we can produce enough food-gains.

Infrastructure Development : Condition of our infrastructure is not at par with the developed nation. We are still behind them. The government of India seems to take care of it. In may vision about infrastructure is that all the cities, towns and metros would be well connected with good road and highways. Transport facilities like bus, train and plane might be available to countryside people. At least 80% of Indian residing in remote villagers may got benefit of infrastructure by 2020.

Defence : Though the good relationship is developing among our neighbours like Pakistan, China, Bangladesh etc.. Yet we need our soil protected by any mischiefs by 2020. I hope our Armed forces will also be counted after the forces of USA & Russia. Our land, sea & Air space would be well protected by our brave soldier. We must have world class state of art missile technology and nuclear capability.

Health and Education : Health and education plays very important role for a developed country. In my opinion by the end of 2020. Our country will call a 100% literate country and no children left without good quality education. It will make my country a developed nations. Besides this, we need to achieve good health to the people. In villages, there is no such facilities for good health. By 2020, every Panchayat must have hospitals with good equipments with doctors and technicians.

Electricity : In these days there are scarcity of electricity and by 2020, every villagers must have electricity not only in day time for industry or for irrigation but also at night. We have to provide wind energy, nuclear energy, solar energy and hydro energy, so that we can produce at least 2 lakh megawatt of electricity .

(ii) Influence of Television Serials on our life

Ans. In the present days television plays an important role in human life. It became a part of the every Indian family. Because about 60% of people passing their time by matching T.V. particularly the female member of the family.

T.V. is a great source of entertainment for us. In T.V. there are so many programme to watch, but the female viewers like the television serials which are daily soap opera for them.

There are number of T.V. serials being broadcasted on T.V and they were liked by the people.

Different type of serials are being aired by number of channels. The social serials related to family matters are very much liked by the people. These daily soap opera influence us very much sometimes good sometimes bad.

Some good influence are:

These serials are generally family based story, which shows the love, care and affection of all the family members who are living together. It has taught the new generation to live and love together. They are able to know the importance of joint-family and their moral values. These serials are also teaching us to respect our moral values, culture and tradition. It also support the mythological term so we are able to know the vast culture of India and respect and adopt it with full of heart.

The serials are familiarising specially the new generation who slowly forget our values, principle, culture and tradition to respect elders and give them the due regards.
The serials are also influence us badly: In the T.V serials, we also watch also many negative character who are trying to harm the family members by their cunning attitude which can sometimes break the families.
The serials also influence the new generation specially the kids by showing the criminal activities and violence, and they eager to do the same action and violence to the others.

Conclusion : after observing all these influences one can easily say that it entirely depend on individual what to adopt or what to not? It is better to adopt the negative attitude but always adopt positive things which enhance the status of an individual in society.

(iii) Computer have turned the word into a global village

Ans. For an increasingly large number of people in this country, especially students, using a computer has become an ordinary and regular part of life and learning. It is almost impossible for us to imagine life without computers, and it's even harder to imagine not having the electricity to use them. Computer has become one of the necessity in the present life. In all spheres, computers are being used and performing the task in a better and quick way. Computer not only increases the speed of work but also the efficiency. Accuracy in work can be attained with the help of computers. Now a days computers are available in each field e.g. banks, railway stations, airports, Government or private offices. Even computers are being used at shopping centres and cinema halls. The day-to-day work in schools and colleges are being done with the help of computers. Big companies are planning their businesses, preparing the estimate of cost-planning, profit and division of work load etc. on the computers itself. The research work and data collection, with great ease, are being done on computers. Now a days, computer is helpful even in simple work like preparation of daily accounts to complicated work like preparing estimates and reports for combining graphic and mathematical data, and can be done by computers quickly.
The computer is being used by students for study and communication purposes. The use of Internet has enabled the young and talented students to find their information from anywhere in the world within a second. The internet facility not only provides students the facility to communicate with people but also study many courses through it. It is a real blessing for the young students. The internet facility provides any type of help whether it is tourism, hotel reservation, ticket reservation, shopping etc. immediately. The use of graphics

has enabled the fashion designers to have new design with great ease. The ATM facility is a new creation of computer technology. People can withdraw cash from ATM any time because it works on twenty four hours basis.
Keeping in mind the above in view, it can be said that we are totally dependent on computers for almost everything and we cannot do anything so easily without computers. Life without computer is like a man sitting in a remote area having no one around him. Computers also help us to keep in touch with almost every new development. Hence I would like to say that life without computers is not possible if a man wants to improve in his life.
After observing all the advantages of computer we can say that computers have turned the world into a global village.

Q7. Read the following passage and summarize it to one-third of its length. Give a suitable title. ***10+2***

We all start life as weak, helpless creatures, totally dependent for both our physical and mental well-being upon those who care for us. It has been demonstrated that, from the very beginning of its separate existence, the baby requires more than simple attention to its physical needs. If a baby is to develop satisfactorily, it is not enough merely to feed it and keep it warm; it needs a mother as a person who will play with it, caress it, and show it affection in all the hundred ways in which mothers do show love towards a child which has been desired and which is welcomed. Babies who are cared for physically, but whose emotional needs are neglected develop more slowly and may, in some instances, suffer permanent damage in that, in adult life, they may never be able to form close emotional ties with any other human being. Every psychiatrist has seen examples of people who were brought up in institutions and who, perhaps, were excellently fed and clothed, but whose emotional needs were left quite unsatisfied. As a result, they grew up into a kind of person who can never keep a friend because the demands which they make upon others are not those of friendship, but rather those of a lost child looking for a parent who can never be found.

Ans. Title – Requirements of a child

Our life begins totally dependent on parents for our separate existence for physical and mental development. Food required for physical need and love, affection, care required for mental and emotional development.
Emotional ties is equally important for complete development of a child, those person who were brought up excellently fed and clothed, but emotionally not satisfied, find themselves difficult for friendship and looked for emotion.

CS-610 : FOUNDATION COURSE IN ENGLISH FOR COMPUTING
June, 2007

Note : Attempt **all** the questions.

1. Read the passage and answer the questions that follow:
VALDARO (ITALY): Italy won't split up its Stone Age "lovers".

In a Valentine's Day gift to the country, scientists said they are determined to remove and preserve together the remains of a couple buried 5,000 to 6,000 years ago, their arms still wrapped around each other in an enduring embrace.

Instead of removing the bones one-by-one for reassembly later, archaeologists plan to scoop up the entire section of earth where the couple was buried, they told Reuters.

The plot will then be transported for study before being put on display in an Italian museum, thereby preserving the world's longest known hug for posterity.

"We want to keep them just as they have been all this time — together," archaeologist Elena Menotti, who announced the discovery a week ago, told Reuters.

Their removal will be a relief for archaeologists who had to hire extra security to guard the rural site outside the northern city of Mantova after the discovery made world headlines.

More importantly, it will give scientists a chance to figure out what has become one of Italian archaeology's greatest mysteries: the first known Neolithic couple to be buried together, hugging. Was it a sudden death? A ritual sacrifice? Or maybe they were prehistoric, star-crossed lovers who took their own lives. That is a crowd-pleasing theory in these parts, since Shakespeare's Romeo and Juliet was set in nearby Verona.

But scientists acknowledge they still know precious little about the now-famous Stone Age couple, whose embrace has become a subject of world newspaper headlines and chat shows. Archaeologists seem certain the

couple died young, since their teeth are intact and that they died during the Stone Age because of an arrowhead and tools found with the remains.

(i) Why does the writer call the embrace of the Stone Age lovers 'enduring'? *2*

Ans. The writer call the embrace of the stone age lovers enduring because the remains of couple buried 5000 to 6000 years ago.

(ii) How do archaeologists plan to preserve the lovers as they are? *1*

Ans. Archaeologists plan to scoop up the entire section of earth where couple was buried.

(iii) Where were the skeletal remains of the lovers found? *1*

Ans. At Valdaro (Italy) the skeletal remains of the lovers were found.

(iv) What are the theories about how the lovers came to be buried together? *3*

Ans. There are three theories about the lovers came to be buried together which are as follows :

– It was sudden death

– A ritual sacrifice

– lovers took their own lives.

(v) What is the connection between Shakespeare's Romeo and Juliet and the lovers in the passage? *2*

Ans. Shakespeare's Romeo and Juliet was set in nearby Verona.

(vi) What other term is used for Stone Age in the write-up? *1*

Ans. Neolithic is the other term which is used for stone age in the write-up.

2. (a) Change the voice.

(i) No one can hold him responsible for the accident. *1*

Ans. He can be hold responsible for the accident by none.

(ii) It is important that we stop all nuclear tests at once. *1*

Ans. All nuclear tests should be stopped at once by us.

(b) Correct the following sentences:

(i) I am not knowing all the facts of the case. *1*

Ans. I don't know all the facts of the case.

(ii) The boss dares not to touch him. *1*

Ans. The boss doesn't have the dare to touch him.

(c) Use the word 'monitor' in two different senses. *2*

Ans. Ram is our class monitor.

District Magistrate is monitoring the disaster management programme.

(d) Use the antonyms of the following words in sentences of your own: radical, negligent *2*

Ans. (i) Radical – Superficial – Despite their superficial similarities the two novels are in fact very different.

(ii) Negligent– meticulousness– She pasted the cutting into scrap book meticulously.

(e) Use the following words in one sentence each to bring out the differences in their meaning: *2*

lose, loose

Ans. India may **lose** the match, if all player not perform well.

The dress was very **loose** to suit her.

3. (a) Use the following phrasal verbs in a sentence of your own: *2*

burn out

fall for

Ans. Burnout – The hotel was completely burnt out, only the walls remained.

Fall for – Rama will never fall for that one.

(b) Fill in the blanks in the following sentences with the correct tense form of the verbs given in brackets:

(i) I __________ (listen) hard out I can't hear anything. *1*

Ans. I **am listening** (listen) hard but I can't hear anything.

(ii) He likes to board the train after it ____________ (start) moving. *1*

Ans. He likes to board the train after it **starts** (start) moving.

(iii) We ___________ (reach) the station just as the train steamed in. *1*

Ans. We **had reached** (reach) the station just as the train steamed in.

4. Write a paragraph of about 150 words on any *one* of the following: 5

(i) The Importance of Being Computer Literate

Ans. Using a computer has become an ordinary and regular part of life and learning. It is almost impossible for us to imagine life without computer.

Computers not only increase the speed of work but also efficiency and accuracy. Now a days computers are available in each field e.g. banks, railways, stations, airports, government offices, private offices, MNC's, BPO's. Even computer being used in shopping mall and cinema halls, the day-to-day academic works and entertainment works.

So, now we understand the importance of computer and to run with the fastest growing era, we should have a very good grip on computer knowledge. We have to be a computer literate. By this field, we can not only make our life easy, but also make our future bright and successful. After being a computer literate, we can easily get a good job, with all the modern facilities and hand some salary. In this era, there is a very vest demand of computer literate to work in various field like MNC's, Bank, BPO's, Government offices, Railways, Airports etc., so it is very important to be a computer literate.

And if we are not a computer literate, then we have to face so many problems, like don't get jobs easily and if you got it after a great struggle, you don't get good salary for making your lifestyle better and future bright.

So, for stand in the present era we have to be a computer literate.

(ii) Bringing up a Girl Child in India

Ans. In India, life of a Girl child has never been an easy life. It may happen that she may not understands her existence. People often hate girls and they do not like a baby girls born in the family.

Many family do not like to educate girls compared to the boys, and mostly girls are get married in very young age.

Every sixth infant girl child dies specifically due to gender discrimination.

So, after knowing all the problems of a girl child, we have to move forward and join our hands together for bringing up a girl child. The girl child must have as equal rights as boy child. Female foetus has been killed by the family with the help of doctors. The right of a girl child starts from womb. Though the Government of India has banned the sex-determination of foetus but yet some doctors secretly do this in human activity. The government must have made some strict law to stop the foetus killing.

Also the society should have to strictly avoid the female foetus killing. But our duties are not end here. We also have to provide them all the benefit which we provide to the boy child. We have to provide her the equal right in-nutrition, health education, respect love and care. And after taking these steps we are able to bring up a girl child and assure the development of family, society and relation.

(iii) Kindness to Animals

Ans. All over the world, the wild life a has been whittled down steadily, and many lovely and interesting animals have been reducing in numbers for want do protection and help. They can never reestablish themselves. In constitution of India under article 51A(G). It shall be the duty of every citizen of India, to protect and improve the natural environment including forests lakes, rivers and wild life and to have composition for living creature. So, it is our fundamental duty to show kindness to animals pet and wild. Few people show kindness to cow, dog for their religion point of view. It is good but we have to show our kindness to other animals also. In circus many animals has kept for our entertainment faced cruelty by their owner. It must be stopped similarly cow slaughter should be banned. Monkeys are the medium of our medical experiments and has faces cruelty by us. Wild animals has been hunted by man for their skin and other value.

There are certain private individuals and some institutions who consider that the work of trying to save and give sanctuary to these hurried animals is very important and they are working in this field.

5. Write an essay of about 300 words on any *one* of the following topics: ***10***

(i) Living in a Small Town

Ans. The soul of our county lives in villages 25% percent of people resides in countryside many of them migrated to metro cities for search of employment and to get many other facilities which is not found in villages. But one should not forget about the thousand of small town in all over the country.

Small town has more facilities than that of village and less facilities than that of big cities and a metropolitan cities. Living in a small town is generally normal. No persons live in a hurry to catch the train, bus or charted. People have enough time to share joy and sorrow with their friends and neighbours. People live simply and qualitative life. There is no pollution and such other problem. If someone wants to round the small town by vehicles, it will take not more than an hour. There is no traffic Jam like big cities or parking problems which generally creates conflict among vehicle owners and commuters. Many small town have food and sufficient school, collage, hospital, entertainment playground. Library etc.. For the people though their things are at par with the big cities, yet people of the town not fully but partially satisfied.
If any mishappening by chance happened, all the person look eager to help the

sufferer and give them support, emotionally as well as financially. In big cities this phenomenon happens no person take care of it only close friends and relatives involves. There is no sympathy from strange person facing any mishappening. So, living in a small town protected strange person by the people. Generally people live peacefully with love, affection and emotionally.

But there is a few misery in small town like, no proper electricity, road, water and quality medical facilities. Local authorities not take care of these things because the political and administrative power are generally live far from the small town and not take serious responsibility to solve their problems. Small town lacking infrastructure development.
But in my opinion, if living in small town is not boon, put at least not a curse also.

(ii) Working in a Call Centre
Ans. The IT-enabled services opportunity in India is expected to cross $20 billion by 2008, according to a recent Nasscom report. Call centre gave rise to the job opportunities of youngsters, college goers with a handsome remunerations.
Working in a call centre is completely extrinsic to country in its focus. Enter any call centre. The English is counted. The dress is getting more and more accounted us well. Be territorial out post of the foreign land beings serviced. Call centre is completely western space. Youngsters under the stress of hormonal pressure are keen to get their own money. The call centre provide an option to earn food, money at a young age, even without degrees in hand. Youth are following an exiting lifestyle at a very–very young age. This is fast trade by money in the hand and the freedom of a working person.

The toyota, qualis revolution is there. Drives are in by demand. There is prosperity all around and call centre is today a sub-culture in itself. Every job profile has its own positive and negative impact.

As far as call centre are concerned, apart from the common work issues like boss, colleagues, target and pressure, the call centre stress is mentally because of working in a shifts and its impact, on the biological, psychological and social life of a individual.

A lot of people working in call centre fall prey of insomania and tend to take sedatives to cure disturbed sleep. Also the tendency to smoke and use of alcohol is prevalent there.
People in call centre due to their different shift cycles tend to get distanced

from their own family and feel stressed.

(iii) The Idea of Being Always the First

Ans. Being always first is an idea which is not always happens. Listening someone getting first in any field. We feel happy and excited but those person who stood first know very well, that how it is difficult. To attain the first is always a challenge for everybody in all prospect of life viz. study, sports, research fields or any competition. Being always the first gives satisfaction, happiness and self respect. To achieve this one must be very careful about few important thing e.g.. Hard Labour:– In any field hard labour which always pays bonus without labour nothing happen. If a student do not study rigorously it would be very difficult for him to retain the first position. Likewise, sportsperson has to do practice hard, so that they couldn't lost game.

Similarly, sincerity in their field is equally important. What is happening in their field in world wide must be know. In the first development of world every technology and science become old in few years and new technology arrives. So, one should very careful and sincere to always get the first.

Honesty always plays a vital role for being always the first. If someone in any field got first by using unfair means they will not get the first position, always. Perhaps, we may even fail rather getting the first position. A person who is honestly prepared for his work, might get first position in any field.

However, there is a negative point also for always being a first particularly in research, discoveries, invention and development field. There are few risk around them not only for their failure but also for their life. Many scientist has already lost their life in space field in Antarctica and in defence research. But who achieve their at first time he become roll model for others. In my points or view, everyone should try their best to always being first but if it somehow not happen, not feel any guilt and depression. It is good idea with lot of research.

6. Read the following passage and summarise it to one-third of its length. Also suggest a suitable title. ***8+2=10***

Mere expansion of the Indian economy will not address the issues relating to the plight of the Indian child who continues to suffer from under-nourishment, anaemia and lack of basic schooling facilities, Nobel Prize winning economist Amartya Sen said here on Tuesday.

The solution to the problem, according to Dr. Sen, may not in radical alternatives but in the classical method of a greater amount of government investment in both education and healthcare, an end to the negligent

attitude towards women and a more collaborative engagement with the various unions. "It is important to see what the government is doing with the extra money that is coming into its coffers," Dr. Sen said.

He cited the example of pre-1979 China, Japan, the U.S. as well as various European countries where public expenditure on education and healthcare had preceded the introduction of reforms aimed at economic expansion.

"The traditional alternative has never been seriously tried in India," Dr. Sen said. The Government of India had not been able to guarantee the right to education as in many parts of the country, there were no functioning schools to attend, he added.

Similarly, the negligent attitude towards women because of the inherent gender bias in society led to undernourished mothers, distressed foetuses and underweight babies. He pointed out that the progress rate has not been very remarkable with undernourishment dropping from 47 to 46 per cent between 1998 – 99 and 2005 – 06 and immunisation coming down from 58 to 56 per cent over the same period.

Ans. **Title Development for child**

Amartya Sen told that though Indian economy is expanding yet children have faced basic problems like under-nourishment, anaemia education etc.

Government investment in education healthcare, empowerment of women and cooperation of unions can solve the problem of children in India.

In various countries the investment on education and healthcare is more than that of expanding economy.

The Indian Government had failed to guarantee the right to education.

He remarked due to gender bias and negligent attitude towards women the progress rate is not remarkable.

CS-610: Foundation Course in English For Computing
December, 2007

Note: Attempt **all** the questions.

Q1. Read the passage and answer the questions the follow:

The Industrial Revolution saw a great increase in the population of Europe. These people wanted goods, tools, clothes, houses and all the things that make civilized life possible. The goods which they wanted had to be fairly cheap, cheap enough to be purchased out of the wages earned in factories or workshops. There were no restrictions on the manufacture of goods as there are in times of war, and each factory competed with its rivals in finding markets for its products. The demand for goods was great, both at home and overseas.

In deciding which goods to buy everyone is influenced by two considerations, price and quality. The ever-increasing demand was for goods of high quality at low prices. That factory and that country prospered whose goods competed successfully with its rivals as regards quality and price. In the nineteenth century, the desire to produce high quality goods at low prices led to, what is now called, mass production. The phrase nowadays is especially associated with the name of Henry Ford, who so successfully applied mass-production methods to the manufacture of motorcars. His business rivals were quick to imitate him, thus proving the truth of the old proverb, 'Imitation is the sincerest form of flattery.' But Mr. Ford was by no means the inventor of mass production. It is difficult, indeed, to say who was. When the first large mills for the manufacture of cloth were built, then, we may say that mass production began. The invention of the steam-engine gave manufacturers the cheap power which they needed. Brilliant men perfected cotton gins and looms. When one huge machine began to perform rapidly the operations previously done slowly and laboriously by hand, the age of mass production was born.

(i) What did the people of Europe want during the time of the Industrial Revolution?

(ii) Why did the Europeans want the goods to be cheap?

(iii) What are the two considerations in deciding which goods to buy?

(iv) What is Henry Ford known for?

(v) Who, in your opinion, invented mass production methods?

Ans. (i) During the time of industrial revolution, the people of Europe were looking for goods, tools, cloths, houses and other necessary things that could make their lives civilized.

(ii)

Ans. They wanted cheap goods because it was the war time, and they were short of money.

(iii)

Ans. There were two considerations, first was the price and second was the quality.

(iv)

Ans. Henry Ford is known for making mass production possible.

(v)

Ans. Henry Ford invented it.

Q2. (a) Rewrite the following sentences in the passive voice:
(i) The female Anopheles mosquito transmits malaria.
(ii) They are going to build a new wing in the administrative block.

Ans. (i) Malaria is transmitted by the female Anopheles mosquito.
(ii) A new wing is being built in administrative block.

(b) Fill in the blanks choosing the suitable option from the ones given in the brackets:
(i) I_______ (had gone, went) to Kashmir last year.
(ii) Lucknow_________ (is, has been) situated on the banks of river Gomti.
(iii) I ________ (am, have been) an early riser since childhood.

Ans. (i) went
(ii) is
(iii) have been

Q3. Rewrite the following sentences removing the error, if any:
(i) You can't get good marks unless you don't work hard.
(ii) Manjeet has always been best cadet of the academy.
(iii) The bunch of keys have been kept on the shelf.
(iv) The travelers were sitting below the shade of the mango tree.
(v) By the time I reached home my mother went to the market.

Ans. (i) You can't get good marks unless you work hard.
(ii) Manjeet has always been the best cadet of the academy.
(iii) The bunch of keys has been kept in the self.
(iv) The travelers were sitting under the mango tree's shade.
(v) By the time I reached home my mother had gone to the market.

Q4. Do as directed:

(i) As soon as I reached the station the train left. (Rewrite using 'no sooner')
(ii) Rita is too weak to run. (Rewrite removing too)
(iii) You are not tired. (Add a question tag)
(iv) Rajni said "Rita, how can you be so cruel to animals?" (Rewrite in indirect speech)
(v) Give the antonyms of the following words:
belief, cruel

Ans. (i) No sooner I reached the station the train left.
(ii) Rita is so weak that she can't run.
(iii) You are not tired. Are you?
(iv) Rajni asked Rita how she could be so cruel to animals.
(v) disbelief, kind

Q5. Write a composition in about 300 words, on any one of the following topics:
(i) Will computers lead to large scale unemployment?
(ii) Population Control: an urgent need
(iii) Deforestation – a big disaster

(i) Will computers lead to large scale unemployment?

Ans. Nothing epitomizes modern life better than the computer. For better or worse, computers have infiltrated every aspect of our society. Today computers do much more than simply compute, supermarket scanners calculate our grocery bill while keeping store inventory; computerized telephone switching centers play traffic cop to millions of calls and keep lines of communication untangled; and automatic teller machines (ATM) let us conduct banking transactions from virtually anywhere in the World. But where did all this technology come from and where is it heading? To fully understand and appreciate the impact computers have on our lives and promises they hold for the future, it is important to understand their evolution.

The history of computers starts out about 2000 years ago, at the birth of the Abacus, a wooden rack holding two horizontal wires with beads strung on them. When these beads are moved around, according to programming rules memorized by the user, all regular arithmetic problems can be done. Another important invention around the same time was the Astrolabe, used for navigation. Blaise Pascal is usually credited for building the first digital computer in 1642. It added numbers entered with dials and was made to help his father, a tax collector. In 1671, Gottfried Wilhelm von Leibniz invented a computer that was built in 1694. It could add, and, after changing some things around, multiply. Leibniz invented a computer that was built in 1694. It could add, and, after changing some things around, multiply. Leibniz invented a special stepped gear mechanism for introducing the addend digits, and this is still being used. The prototypes made by Pascal and Leibniz were not used in many places, and considered weird until a little more than a century later, when Thomas of Colmar created the first successful mechanical calculator that could add, subtract, multiply and divide. A lot of improved desktop calculators by many inventors followed, so that by about 1890, the range of improvements such as Accumulation of partial results; Storage and automatic entry of past results and Printing of the results were included. But each of these required manual installation. These improvements were mainly made for commercial users, and not for the needs of science.

The computer development was grown on year by year by the works of many brilliants. The saturation level of computer was reached after one and half centuries i.e., in 1981, IBM introduced its personal computer (PC) for use in the home, office and schools. The 1980's saw an expansion in computer use in all three arenas as clones of the IBM PC made the personal computer even more affordable. The numbers of personal computers in use more than doubled from 2 million in 1981 to 5.5 million in 1982. Ten years later, 65 million PCs were being used. Computer continued their trend toward a smaller size, working their way down from desktop to laptop computers, which could fit inside a briefcase to palmtop, able to fit inside a breast pocket. In direct competition with IBM's PC was Apple's Macintosh line, introduced in 1984. Notable for its user-friendly design, the Macintosh offered an operating system that allowed users to move screen icons instead of typing instructions. Users controlled the screen cursor using a mouse, a device that mimicked the movement of one's hand on the computer screen.

As computer became more widespread in the workplace, new ways to harness their potential developed. As smaller computers became more powerful, they could be linked together, or networked, to share memory space, software and information and communicate with each other. As opposed to a mainframe computer, which was one powerful computer that shared time with many terminals for many applications, networked computers allowed individual computers to form electronic co-ops. Using either direct wiring, called a Local Area Network (LAN), or telephone lines, these networks could reach enormous proportions. A global web of computer circuity, the Internet, for example, links computers worldwide into a single network of informations. The widespread use of the computers in every area may become one of the reason to increase the problem of unemployment. As the work done manually by many employees can be done easily with one computer and one computer operator.

(ii) Population Control: an urgent need

Ans. The demographic transition in the developed countries occurred without a government sponsored family planning programme. The Transition took place in a synchronized manner along with socio-economic development. The rate of growth of their population was never very high. The experience of the developing countries, in this respect, was rather skewed. After the Second World War, these countries experienced a sudden decline in mortality, which was devoid of, in most cases, any perceptible improvement in socio-economic development. Before the level of fertility started declining, they attained a low level of mortality, which was comparable to that existing in developed countries when they were completing the transition. For the developing countries, the growth rates have sometimes crossed the 3 percent mark.

India, along with other South and South-East Asian countries, faced a similar demographic situation at the initial stage of transition. A woman had, on an average, six children and average life expectancy was 40 years at the beginning of 1950. India pioneered the effort to control population in the early fifties, the other countries in the reason like China, Korea, Thailand, Indonesia and Sri Lanka, though introduced government sponsored family planning programmes much later, have progressed far ahead of India in achieving their goal of fertility reduction.

High rates of infant, child and maternal mortality in India are generally symptomatic for the poor nutritional and health status of the majority of the population. Infant deaths are the result of many factors such as poor nutrition of pregnant mothers, which is associated with low birth weight babies who have very high risk of dying, inadequate care during pregnancy, and unhygienic conditions during delivery. Permanent reductions in infant, child and maternal mortality rates will occur only when the overall hygiene and living standards of the population improves substantially.

India entered the 21st century with close to a billion people, the majority of whom lack even the basic amenities necessary for a healthy and dignified existence. Future government will be challenged by the task for providing employment and minimal living standards for nearly seventeen percent of the global population. The task is rendered more difficult by a relatively rapid rate of population growth that results in the addition of nearly 20 million to the population every year.

Although India started its official family planning program way back in 1951, a formal statement on population policy was issued by the Congress Government in 1976 when India passing through Internal Emergency. In 1977, second population policy statement was issued by the Janata Government, retaining some of the measures proposed by the 1976 policy and departing from other significant measures. In 1986, third population policy statement was issued by the Congress Government. But it never saw the light of the day.

In July 1993, the Government of India constituted an Expert Group on Population Policy under the Chairmanship of Dr. M.S. Swaminathan. The Expert Group has submitted its report called "Draft National Population Policy" in May 1994. The strengths and weaknesses of the population policies and arrives at the inescapable conclusion that the Draft National Population Policy submitted by the Expert Group provides a congenial environment to achieve "a stable population with a satisfying standard of life for all".

The programme in India is geared by increasing allocation of resources in each successive plan. Many innovative strategies and programmes have been introduced from time to time to give it a new direction. No doubt the level of fertility has declined, but it has been too slow. There is a need to have a comprehensive review of the birth control policy in India as it has developed over the fast five decades. Such an assessment can provide insights to shape the future policy in the country.

(iii) Deforestation – a big disaster

Ans. Deforestation means converting forested areas to non-forest land for use such as arable land, pasture, urban use, logged area, or wasteland. Generally, the removal or destruction of significant areas of forest cover has resulted in a degraded environment with reduced biodiversity. In many countries, massive deforestation is ongoing and is shaping climate and geography. Djouce Mountain, along with most of the island of Ireland, was systematically clear felled during the 17th and 18th centuries, in order to obtain wood mainly for shipbuilding. Jungle burned for agriculture in southern Mexico. Since about the mid-1800s the Earth has experienced an unprecedented rate of change of destruction of forests worldwide. Forests in Europe are adversely affected by acid rain and very large areas of Siberia have been harvested since the collapse of the Soviet Union. In the last two decades, Afghanistan has lost over 70% of its forests throughout the country. However, it is in the world's great tropical rainforests where the destruction is most pronounced at the current time and where wholesale felling is having an adverse effect on biodiversity and contributing to the ongoing Holocene mass extinction. About half of the mature tropical forests, between 750 to 800 million hectares of the original 1.5 to 1.6 billion hectares that once covered the planet have fallen. The forest loss is already acute in [Southeast Asia], the second of the world's great biodiversity hot spots. Much of what remains is in the, where the covered more than 600 million hectares. The forests are being destroyed at an accelerating pace tracking the rapid pace of human population growth. Unless significant measures are taken on a world-wide basis to preserve them, by 2030 there will only be ten percent remaining with another ten percent in a degraded condition. 80 percent will have been lost and with them the irreversible loss of hundreds of thousands of species. Many tropical countries, including Indonesia, Thailand, Malaysia, Bangladesh, China, Sri Lanka, Laos, Nigeria, Liberia, Guinea, Ghana and the Cote d'Ivoire have lost large areas of their rainforest. 90% of the forests of the Philippine archipelago have been cut. In 1960 Central America still had 4/5 of its original forest; now it is left with only 2/5 of it. Madagascar has lost 95% of its rainforests. Atlantic coast of Brazil has lost 90-95% of its Mata Atlantica rainforest. Half of the Brazilian state of Rondonia's 24.3 million hectares have been destroyed or severely degraded in recent years. As of 2007, less than 1% of Haiti's forests remain, causing many to call Haiti's Caribbean desert. Between 1990 and 2005, the Nigeria lost a staggering 79% of its old-growth forests. Several countries, notably the Philippines, Thailand and India have declared their deforestation activity a very serious national threat.

Q6. Summarize the following passage in 150 words:

For thousands of years, dreams have interested, puzzled and even frightened people. It used to be thought that dreams always came true. People thought that the figures appearing in dreams were messengers from the gods and that special kinds of dreams had special meanings. A dream of flowers might mean good luck.

Since the end of the 19th century, physicians, psychologists, and other scientists have been studying dreams. Although they still have much to learn, today they believe that dreams do not appear from some mysterious place outside the person, Rather, they think that the dreamer creates dreams himself. There are two kinds of dreaming: day dreaming, which is done while the dreamer is awake, and night dreaming, which is done while he is asleep. Both day dreams and night dreams occur when the dreamer is so relaxed that he pays no attention to what goes on around him. Then his thoughts can wander wherever they want. For this reasons, both sorts of dreams are often about strange persons, animals or situations, which could not possibly exist, in real life. Night dreams are even more unusual and unrealistic than day dreams, because in sleep people have almost no control over what they think.

Although nearly anything may appear in a dream, there are certain sorts of dreams which almost, everybody has. Most persons, at sometime or other, have dreams in which their dearest wish is granted, or in which they become somebody they would like to be. A boy or a girl who is bored in school may daydream that he or she is out fishing or playing ball. A woman who is tired of doing housework may daydream that she is a famous singer and she may become so lost in her dream that she does not hear the doorbell. All persons whether they are children or adults, wish and hope for things they cannot have. Many persons get these

things in dreams....

Most persons occasionally dream they are being chased by robbers, or are falling or are in danger of fire or flood. These are frightening dreams. Children's frightening dreams are likely to contain witches, ghosts, or animals that bite. These very frightening dreams are called nightmares. People usually have nightmares when they are frightened or upset about something in their lives.

Ans. Usually it is believed by the people that dreams are always come true and they are the messages sent by the god. It is believed that each dreams has a special meaning like flowers represents to good luck. Since the end of the 19th century, physicians, psychologists, and other scientists have been studying dreams. There are two kinds of dreaming: day dreaming and nigh dreaming, which happened during the awake and asleep, occurred during the relaxation. A boy or a girl who is bored in school may daydream that he or she is fishing or playing ball and a man or woman may daydream that he/she is a famous singer. Some dreams occurred occasionally, like chasing by robbers, falling, fires or flood, which known as frightening dreams. Children's frightening dreams are often have witches, ghosts or animals that give bitings.

CS – 610: FOUNDATION COURSE IN ENGLISH FOR COMPUTING
June, 2008

*Note: Attempt **all** the questions.*

Q1. Read the passage and answer the questions that follow:
'Tax avoidance' and 'tax evasion' are terms so frequently referred to in economic and business relationships today that they constitute part of our conversational language and people in general use these terms even without knowing their exact meaning and difference. Whereas tax avoidance implies a situation in which the taxpayer reduces his tax liability by taking advantage of the loop-holes and ambiguities in the legal provisions, in the case of tax evasion, facts are deliberately misinterpreted and the tax liability is understand. Thus, while tax avoidance is perfectly legal and is, at times, referred to as 'tax planning', tax evasion is illegal and, therefore, carries with it the risk of penalties and prosecutions under the tax laws. As such, the black economy comprises the sum total of all the various methods of tax *evasion* but does not include *tax avoidance*. Accordingly, whereas the consequences of the two phenomena are different for the taxpayers, both reduce the revenue of the exchequer and consequently need to be checked to the greatest extent possible.
The unsanctioned or black market economy is created due to evasion of both direct and indirect taxes, undervaluation of properties, anti-social activities like smuggling, foreign exchange racketeering, under-invoicing and over-invoicing of foreign trade, remittances from abroad through illegal channels, etc.

(a) Say whether the following statements are true *(T)* or false *(F)*:
(i) Tax evasion helps in generating black money.
(ii) Both tax evasion and tax avoidance are illegal.
Ans. (i) True (ii) False

(b) How do taxpayers take advantage of the loop-holes in tax laws?
Ans. By taking advantages from loop-holes the taxpayer reduces his tax liability.

(c) Write another phrase for *tax avoidance*.
Ans. Tax Planning = Tax avoidance.

(d) Why does the writer think that both tax avoidance and tax evasion should be checked?

Ans. They should be checked because they give rise to black economy.

(e) Give the antonyms of *liability* and *ambiguity*.

Ans. liability – assets
ambiguity – univocal

(f) Explain the phrases *conversational language* and *revenue of the exchequer*.

Ans. (i) Conversational language: It is the language in which the transactions are done.

(ii) Revenue of exchequer: It is the cash collection in terms of tax by the government.

(g) Give the singular of *phenomena*.

Ans. phenomenon

Q2. (a) Correct the following sentences:
(i) I have finished reading the novel yesterday.
(ii) Earth revolves round the Sun.

Ans. (i) I finished reading the novel yesterday.
(ii) The earth revolves round the Sun.

(b) Change the voice:
(i) Cigarettes are not sold here.
(ii) The new Girls' Hostel was inaugurated by the Vice-Chancellor.

Ans. (i) We do not sell cigarettes.
(ii) The Vice-Chancellor inaugurated the new Girls' Hostel.

(c) Use the given phrasal verbs in sentences of your own:
put off, look down on

Ans. Put off: Students **put off** their uniforms after school.
Down on: In America, still the white look **down on** the black.

(d) Use the following words in two separate sentences to bring out the difference in their meaning :
respectful, respectable

Ans. Respectful: He is a **respectful** person in society.
Respectable: You have done a good job. Your work is **respectable**.

(e) Write the antonyms of the following words and use them (antonyms) in meaningful sentences:
latter, pessimist

Ans. Latter – subsequent
What are the subsequent results of this process.
Pessimist – optimist
Mr. Verma is a great **optimistic** he sees white phase of everything.

Q3. (a) Combine the following sentences into a single sentence, using *no sooner…than*:

1. We reached the station.

2. The train steamed in.

Ans. No sooner we reached the station than the train steamed in.

(b) Fill in the blanks with the correct form of the tense of the verbs given in brackets:

(i) I __________ (work) very hard since morning.

(ii) If you had worked hard you __________ (get) good marks.

Ans. (i) have been working

(ii) would get

(c) Complete the sentence with a suitable question tag:

You have read the novel, __________?

Ans. haven't you

Q4. Write a paragraph of about 150 words on any *one* of the following:

(i) English as a Global language

Ans. The world is a big and large place. There are more than ten thousands of local languages in the word. Only in our country India we have more than one hundred local languages. So in such a situation how can be it possible that the people contact each other very easily? Even in our country we cannot communicate. We have a saying here that in India language changes on every mile. In such a critical situation we need a language that can make us global, that we can understand the world around us, that we can live easily. What else can serve us better than 'English'?

It is a talk nowadays that India is trying to eliminate English from all walks of life in order to develop its national language, which is shaken for those who are spending millions of dollars every month on learning English. In Iran, Persian is their national language and it is a progressive language. Their medium of instruction, administration and entertainment are in Persian. Even intellectuals depend upon it. Hardly ten percent can speak English fluently. No foreigner can stay for long without proficiency in local languages. Yet, in the oil-rich developing country, all the senior positions are automatically held by those who can speak in English. In India, we have innumerous languages. They are not mostly inter-linked each other. Only the English brought by the Britishers' is the medium of interconnection among us. So, it is not the fair way that English is the foreign language and it should be abandoned. It is not wise to nourish our own mother, giving trouble to some other mother.

(ii) Email has replaced letter writing as a mode of personal communication

Refer to Page-56, Topic (ii)

(iii) Use of computers in education

Refer to Page-163, Topic (iii)

Q5. Write an essay of about 300 words on any *one* of the following:

(i) Cyber Crime

Refer to Page-143, Q4(i)

(ii) Advantages and disadvantages of Shopping over the Internet

Ans. The rapid development of information and communication technologies over the past decade has revolutionized business practices. Technology has an interesting relationship with commerce.

One of the most promising facets of global connectivity has been **E-commerce. E-commerce** has made its presence felt through some good sites like ***MumbaiMart*** and ***Rediff***. While Rediff has made significant inroads into achieving customer loyalty by addressing varied avenues like movie tickets and music, MumbaiMart has been launched for its product and service galleries, payment options and delivery times. Favourites apart, the issue at hand remains the huge amounts of sales that can be achieved through a web-based showroom. Tele shopping has been around for some time now and has worked in the favour of **e-commerce** by easing the consumer's mind into the idea of shopping from home.

E-commerce is not only the buying and selling of goods and services on the Internet, especially the World Wide Web but can be divided into.

E-Business is what happens when you combine the broad reach of the Internet with vast resources of traditional information technology systems. It uses the Web to connect together customers, vendors, suppliers and employees in a way never before possible. They do business on the Web and consequently they do more business.

Electronic Data Interchange (EDI): It is a standard format for exchanging business data. EDI is one form of e-commerce that also includes e-mail and fax. EDI data exchange among parties that know each other well and make arrangements for one-to-one connection usually dial-up.

E-mail: Companies can use very simple tools such as the e-mail to carry out e-commerce. This form is used mainly for business-to-business transactions. But with more and more people connecting to the Internet, the companies are now also targeting the consumers. E-mail is used mostly for the purpose of sales promotion and advertising. A number of business Web sites offer e-mail newsletters for subscribers. The newsletters may carry product information, product updates or even news pertaining to the product range.

E-retailing or the Virtual Storefront: You can buy anything from you vegetables to your electronic items via the Web browser. This has been made possible all thinks to the evolution of **e-retailing**. Shopping on the Internet is getting common due to various advantages such as 24-hour availability, a global reach, the ability to interact and provide custom information and ordering and it's multimedia prospects. Besides all these plus points the most important factor today for a buyer is the "price". Shopping is not the only attraction on the Net. Other services like booking theatre tickets or even airline tickets, hotel rooms are also being well accepted by the people and is looking forward for more of such services.

In India e-commerce is still a relatively unknown and unused entity, but with the government's open attitude towards progression the cyber-laws concerned will soon be formulated. At the India Internet World held at New Delhi, industry experts expected e-commerce in India to reach $160 million by the year 2001 if leased line costs drop sharply. This would enable more companies to setup their virtual stores on the Internet at cheaper rates.

Though the rapid development of information and communication technologies over the past decade has revolutionized business practices, transactions accomplished through electronic means-collectively "electronic commerce" have created new legal issues. The shift from paper-based to electronic transactions has raised questions concerning the recognition, authenticity and enforceability of electronic documents and signatures. The challenge for lawmakers has been to balance the sometimes-conflicting goals of safeguarding electronic commerce and encouraging technological development.

There is a negative side also while entertaining E-commerce trade. Electronic commerce will have an enormous impact on children's lives. The Internet will provide children with many new opportunities for learning, civic engagement, community building and new forms of creativity. New forms of electronic media may also have potentially negative effects on children's lives. For example, the Internet, Digital Television and other forms of electronic media allow for the "one-to-one" targeted marketing.

Children, particularly younger children, are more vulnerable to advertising and commercial messages. Small children also have difficulties distinguishing between advertising and programming. Other studies suggest negative effects of food, alcohol and tobacco advertising to children on public health. Further, many parents and consumer groups are concerned with the impact of advertising on the development of children's values, particularly materialism. Children must be able to take advantage of the benefits of new digital media in a safe environment. Data collectors should not collect personal information from children unless it is relevant, necessary and lawful. Parents should be involved when data are collected from young children. Therefore, data collectors must be required to obtain parental consent prior to data collection from young children.

Advertising and promotions targeted at children should be clearly identifiable as such and separated from content. There should be limitations on advertising to children, for example with regard to the products or the manner in which they are sold or promoted. Business should not take advantage of children's credulity and lack of experience.

Electronic commerce raises profound and fundamental challenges to national policies that seek to restrict parallel imports of goods. Considering all the above, the Ministry of Commerce has initiated to prepare a draft of Electronic Commerce Act and Electronic Commerce Support Act to facilitate a secure regulatory environment for Electronic Commerce. Though there is a long time before the World becomes a place where digital cash becomes the only mode of payment and shopping means setting into our favourite, chair with our notebook connected to the Internet over a wireless, high-speed link, lets be glad that the wheels have finally started turning the right way.

(iii) The Computer Revolution

Ans. Nothing epitomizes modern life better than the computer. For better or worse, computers have infiltrated every aspect of our society. Today computers do much more than simply compute, supermarket scanners calculate our grocery bill while keeping store inventory; computerized telephone switching centers play traffic cop to millions of calls and keep lines of communication untangled and automatic teller machines (ATM) let us conduct banking transactions from virtually anywhere in the World. But where did all this technology come from and where is it heading? To fully understand and appreciate the impact computers have on our lives and promises they hold for the future, it is important to understand their evolution.

The history of computers starts out about 2000 years ago, at the birth of the **Abacus**, a wooden rack holding two horizontal wires with beads strung on them. When these beads are moved around, according to programming rules memorized by the user, all regular arithmetic problems can be done. Another important invention around the same time was the **Astrolabe,** used for navigation.

Blaise Pascal is usually credited for building the first **digital** computer in 1642. It added numbers entered with dials and was made to help his father, a tax collector. In 1671, Gottfried Wilhelm von Leibniz invented a computer that was built in 1694. It could add and after changing some things around, multiply. Leibniz invented a special **stepped gear mechanism** for introducing the addend digits and this is still being used.

The prototypes made by Pascal and Leibniz were not used in many places and considered weird until a little more than a century later, when Thomas of Colmar created the first successful mechanical calculator that could add, subtract, multiply and divide. A lot of improved desktop calculators by many inventors followed, so that by about 1890, the range of improvements such as Accumulation of partial results; Storage and automatic reentry of past results and Printing of the results were included. But each of these required manual installation. These improvements were mainly made for commercial users and not for the needs of science.

While Thomas of Colmar was developing the desktop calculator a series of very interesting developments in computers was started in Cambridge, England, by Charles Babbage, a mathematics professor. In 1812, Babbage realized that many long calculations, especially those needed to make mathematical tables, were really a series of predictable actions that were constantly repeated. From this he suspected that it should be possible to do these automatically.

He began to design an automatic mechanical calculating machine in 1822, which the called a difference engine. The difference engine, although having limited adaptability and applicability, was really a great advance. Babbage continued to work on if for the next 10 years, but in 1833 he lost interest because he thought he had a **better idea** the construction of what would now be called a general purpose, fully program controlled, automatic mechanical digital computer.

The plans for this engine required an identical decimal computer operating on numbers of 50 decimal digits (or words) and having a storage capacity (memory) of 1,000 such digits. The built-in operations were supposed to include everything that a modern general purpose computer would need, even the all important **Conditional Control Transfer Capability** that would allow commands to be executed in any order, not just the order in which they were programmed.

The computer development was grown on year by year by the works of many brilliants. The saturation level of computer was reached after one and half centuries i.e., in 1981, IBM introduced its personal computer (PC) for use in the home, office and schools. The 1980s saw an expansion in computer use in all three arenas as clones of the IBM PC made the personal computer even more affordable. The number of personal computers in use more than doubled from 2 million in 1981 to 5.5 million in 1982. Ten years later, 65 million PCs were being used. Computer continued their trend toward a smaller size, working their way down from desktop to laptop computers, which could fit inside a briefcase to palmtop, able to fit inside a breast pocket. In direct competition with IBM's PC was Apple's Macintosh line, introduced in 1984. Notable for its user-friendly design, the Macintosh offered an operating system that allowed users to move screen icons instead of typing instructions. Users controlled the screen cursor using a mouse, a device that mimicked the movement of one's hand on the computer screen.

As computer became more widespread in the workplace, new ways to harness their potential developed. As smaller computers became more powerful, they could be linked together or networked, to share memory space, software and information and communicate with each other. As opposed to a mainframe computer, which was one powerful computer that shared time with many terminals for many applications, networked computers allowed individual computers to form electronic co-ops. Using either direct wiring, called a Local Area Network (LAN) or telephone lines, these networks could reach enormous proportions. A global web of computer circuity, the Internet, for example, links computers worldwide into a single network of information.

Q6. Read the following passage and summarise it to one-third of its length; give a suitable title also.
People of different nations first began to trade with one another because some countries were able to produce certain goods which others, because of climatic and geographical differences, could not. Differences of soil and climate restrict the cultivation of many crops to particular regions of the world, while for geological reasons some minerals are found in very few areas of the world. These regional and physical differences provided a basis for international trade once satisfactory means of transporting goods from one place to another had been developed. Since from very early times costs of transportation were very high because of heavy losses in transit, the commodities that were first to enter into international trade were generally fairly valuable articles. For a long time only the rich, anywhere in the world, could afford to buy imported goods.

As means of transport improved and transit risks decreased — and those that remained came to be covered by insurance — international trade gradually expanded. The greatest expansion in trade occurred, however, when countries began to find it to their advantage to specialize in the production of a limited range of goods which they could produce more plentifully and more cheaply than other countries.

Ans. Title: Expansion of International Trade
The trade between nations first began because what one could produce others could not, due to geographical differences. It affected the cropping throughout the world. Some minerals are in abundance at one place while there is none at other. And with the developing of good transport this international trade began to develop. In the beginning the transportation cost was high so only valuable items were dealt in. When the risk factor decreased and the insurance came into existence the trade widened. This trade expanded greatly when many countries began to produce only the things that they could produce in plenty.

CS – 610: FOUNDATION COURSE IN ENGLISH FOR COMPUTING
Dec, 2008

*Note: Attempt **all** the questions.*

Q1. Read the passage given below and answer the questions that follow it:

All around us we see that differences are growing. People shout and fight for the most trivial of reasons. But differences can lead to wars, so they cannot be ignored for long. Different people handle differences differently.

Some shun differences; they are afraid of them. It disturbs them that someone may have a different skin colour, worship a different god or follow a different lifestyle. They are convinced that their way of life is the best and the only way. They enjoy ridiculing those who are different and they don't hesitate to fight to prevent others from following their way. They often join gangs or anti-groups because there is strength in numbers.

There are others, however, who are tolerant of differences. Their motto is 'you keep to yourself and I'll keep to myself'. They don't threaten but they also don't embrace difference.

The third group, celebrators, value difference. They seem them as an advantage, not as a weakness. They have learnt that two people who think differently can achieve more than two people who think alike. They realize that celebrating differences doesn't mean that you necessarily agree with or adopt these differences.

(a) Say whether the following statements are true (T) or false (F):

(i) People fight only when there are serious problems.

(ii) We cannot ignore differences for a long time.

Ans. (i) False

(ii) True

(b) Mention *any two* things that disturb the people who do not like differences.

Ans. (1) Skin colour

(2) Worshipping different gods

(c) Why do the people who hate differences often join anti-groups?

Ans. They join because there is strength in number.

(d) What do you understand by 'you keep to yourself and I'll keep to myself'?

Ans. It means don't meddle in other's matter.

(e) Complete the following sentences with an appropriate word/phrase from the passage (para 4):

(i) There are some people who value differences.

(ii) Celebrating differences doesn't mean that we necessarily **agree with these differences.**

Q2. (a) Rewrite the following sentences in the passive voice:

(i) They didn't invite him to their party last week.

Ans. He wasn't invited by them to their party last week.

(ii) Alexander Bell invented the telephone in 1876.

Ans. Telephone was invented by Alexander Bell in 1876.

(b) Fill in the blanks, choosing the suitable option from the ones given in brackets:

(i) They aren't rich. They haven't **(haven't, don't) got much money.**

(ii) We can walk to their station from here. It isn't **(isn't, don't) very far.**

(iii) I haven't **(don't, haven't) seen him for a long time.**

Q3. Rewrite the following sentences, removing the errors in them:

(a) I was hungry but there wasn't nothing to eat.

Ans. I was hungry but there wasn't anything to eat.

(b) I feel good; I sleep very well last night.

Ans. I feel good; I slept very well last night.

(c) Somebody has broken this window last night.

Ans. Somebody broke this window last night.

(d) Where were your shoes make?

Ans. Where were your shoes made?

(e) What time did you got home last night?

Ans. What time did you get home last night?

Q4. Do as directed:

(a) He is very young. He won't understand this story. (Rewrite as a single sentence, using 'too'.)

Ans. He is too young to understand this story.

(b) He was the first person to congratulate me on my promotion. (Use 'who'.)

Ans. He was the first person who congratulated me on my promotion.

(c) He is very tired. He can't work. (Combine the sentences using 'so...that'.)

Ans. He is so tired that he can't work.

(d) He is a good painter. He sometimes paints bad pictures. (Combine the sentence using 'although'.)

Ans. He sometimes paints bad pictures though he is a good painter.

(e) Passing by the post office, would you please buy some stamps for me? (Change the underlined phrase into a 'when' clause.)

Ans. When you pass by a post office, would you please buy some stamps for me?

Q5. Write a composition, in about 300 words, on *any one* of the following topics:

(a) Computers have revolutionized the modern workplace.

Refer to June-2009, Q.No.-5(c)

(b) Growing incidence of violence against the elderly people.

Ans. Violence against the elderly includes physical, sexual and psychological abuse as well as neglect, says the report. Elderly people are also vulnerable to economic abuse with others making unscrupulous use of their resources. Information on the extent of abuse against the elderly is scant and the few population-based studies that have been conducted suggest that about four to six per cent of old people have experienced some form of abuse at home. The elderly are also at risk in institutions such as hospitals, nursing homes and other long-term care facilities. In a survey undertaken in the USA, 36 per cent of nursing home staff reported having witnessed at least one incident of physical abuse of an elderly patient in the previous year. Ten per cent admitted having committed at least one act of physical abuse themselves and 40 per cent said they had psychologically abused old patients.

The WHO report cautions that the consequences of abuse of the elderly are especially serious, because of their fragility. Their bones are more brittle and injuries take longer to heal. Even a relatively minor injury can cause serious and permanent damage. The risk factors for such abuse are aggravated by strained family relationships that could worsen because of feelings of frustration, as the older person becomes more dependent and therefore, a greater burden. The report cites social isolation as a significant reason for an older person being subjected to mistreatment. Many elderly people are isolated either because of physical or mental infirmities or through the loss of friends and family members.

A poser levelled by an elderly participant at the recent discussion in Delhi best sums up the situation. When he asked, could senior citizens just relax on their own lawns without fearing for their safety? There are no easy answers, but public education and awareness are powerful instruments in preventing abuse and neglect of the elderly. The WHO report says that educational programmes aimed at older people are usually more successful if the information on abuse is woven into wider topics such as successful aging or health care.

(c) Food adulteration – a crime against humanity.

Ans. DEFINITION: Adulteration is defined as the process by which the quality or the nature of a given substance is reduced through the addition of a foreign or an inferior substance and the removal of a vital element.

TYPES OF ADULTERANTS: Intentional, and Incidental

Intentional: Intentional adulterants are those substances that are added as a deliberate act on the part of the adulterer with the intention to increase the margin of profit. E.g. sand, marble chips, stones, mud, chalk powder, water, dyes, etc., These adulterants cause harmful effects on the body.

Incidental: These adulterants are found in food substances due to ignorance, negligence or lack of proper facilities. It is not a willful act on the part of the adulterer. E.g. pesticides, droppings of rodents, larvae in food.

The conventional methods of packing which are prevalent even now to a large extent are tin or aluminium containers, glass bottles and jars, paper and waxed paper wrappings, paper cartons, cardboard and certain plastic containers. Tin and aluminium containers have become costly and glass bottles though very good in many respects have problems associated with breakage and heavy transportation charges on account of weight. Continued use of paper in increased volume dwindles the natural resources. Polystyrene is principally made into tubs for ice creams, packs for eggs, sausages and small packages for butter, jam and cheese. Bags made from the simplest of all plastic polymers, namely, polyethylene or 'polythene' as commonly known have relatively low preserving qualities. Material such as polyesters vinyl acetate derivatives and multilayer films made out of a combination of different materials have good preserving characteristics for food products.

Shrink wrap packaging is a system where heat shrinkable thermoplastic film is wrapped around an article or a group of articles. The film is made to shrink around it by the application of heat to achieve a skin light package. Canned food products, bottles and jars of all types can be shrink wrapped.

Now-a-days it is expected that packaging material be environment friendly or ecofriendly, that is, it should not pose many problems for mankind and hazards to the environment.

For example, corrugated boxes are ecofriendly and are preferred for exporting. They can be effectively replaced for conventional wooden boxes which need to destroy the trees. Recyclability of packaging is desirable so as to preserve the resources of the packaging material for future generations.

Plastics such as cellulose acetate, polyamide polyethylene polypropylene and polyvinyl chloride are often used as packing materials because they are light in weight and are resistant to diffusion due to solvents and high temperatures. However care should be taken that only food grade plastic packing materials should be used for packaging foods to prevent the following packaging hazards.

Q6. Summarise the following passage in about 120 words:

Most people believe that children are the world's most valuable resource and should be loved and cherished. However, because they are dependent on adults for safety and nurturing, they are often treated badly and abused. A report published by the World Health Organisation (WHO) in 1999 claimed that more than 40 million children around the world suffer from abuse and maltreatment.

But things are beginning to change. Did you know that the United Nations has a special convention on the Rights of the Child and that Article 19 and Article 34 of this Convention deal specifically with child abuse?

Child abuse has been defined as 'all forms of physical and/or emotional treatment or commercial or other exploitation, resulting in actual or potential harm to the child's right to health, survival, development or dignity in the context of a relationship of responsibility, trust or power'. It is being increasingly recognized that even children deserved to be treated with dignity and that their freedom should be respected. From the year 2000, 20th November is celebrated as the International Day for the Rights of the Child and 19th November is World Day for the Prevention of Child Abuse.

Ans. Children are widely believed to be the richest resource of the world. That should be preserved. But they are treated oddly sometimes. In 1999, WHO Report claimed that over 40 million children suffer maltreatment every year.

But with the time things have changed. The UNO has a special convention under article 19 and 34 against child abuse. They have defined the child abuse clearly. All forms of physical and emotional maltreatment falls under it. A child has been given right to live free healthy life. 20th November has been firced to be celebrated as Day for the Rights of the Child and 19th of November for Preservation of Child Abuse.

CS – 610: FOUNDATION COURSE IN ENGLISH FOR COMPUTING
June, 2009

*Note: Attempt **all** the questions.*

Q1. Read the passage and answer the questions that follow:

Since the introduction of wide spread vaccination programmes, millions of people have been protected against potentially fatal diseases and countless lives have been saved.

Vaccines prepare your immune system to fight disease by taking advantage of the fact that the immune system can "remember" infections organisms. Vaccination gives us immunity without having to experience the disease or its symptoms.

Each vaccine contains a killed or weakened form of the organism (usually a virus or a bacterium) that causes a particular disease. Even though the organism in the vaccine has been altered so that it would not make you ill, the part of the organism that stimulates your immune system to respond is still present. This is the antigen.

An antigen is any substance that is recognized as foreign and stimulates the production of anti-bodies, for example an antigen may be a foreign protein on the surface of the bacterium. An antigen specifically induces the production of anti-bodies which can bind to neutralize it.

After you have been vaccinated, some of the cells that are responsible for protecting you against disease your B lymphocytes – detect the antigens in the vaccine. The B lymphocytes will react as if the real infections organism was invading your body they multiply to form an army of identical cells that are able to respond to the antigens in the vaccine. The cloned cells then evolve into one of two types of cells: plasma cells or memory B cells.

(a) How do vaccines help us to remain healthy?

Ans. Vaccine prepare our immune system to fight diseases because immune system can remember the infection organisms.

(b) What is an antigen? Where would you find it?

Ans. An antigen is any substance as a foreign body and it stimulates the production of anti-bodies. It is found inside an organism.

(c) How does the vaccine stimulate our immune system?

Ans. Vaccines improve our immune system by creating the antigens that out against anti bodies.

(d) Provide the antonym of the words 'altered' and 'responsible'.

Ans. altered – unaltered, **responsible** – irresponsible

(e) Explain the terms:
(i) symptom
Ans. Symptoms are the signs of something such as diseases etc.
(ii) fatal
Ans. Fatal means something that causes death.
(iii) stimulate
Ans. Stimulates means to increase the rate of something.
(iv) multiply
Ans. Multiply means the increase in number rapidly by itself.
(f) Pick word from the passage which mean the following:
(i) cells responsible for protecting us against disease
Ans. lymphocytes
(ii) communicable and transferable
Ans. infectious
(iii) develop, grow
Ans. multiply
(iv) molecules which are trained to in activate an organism
Ans. antigen

Q2. (a) Correct the following sentences:
(i) We are fearing that our candidate may not win.
Ans. We fear that our candidate may not win.
(ii) I have obtained my degree in 1997.
Ans. I had obtained my degree in 1997.
(b) Complete the following sentences using appropriate Prepositional Phrase:
(i) This letter is in appropriate __________ to the established norms.
(ii) My country has stringent immigrated laws __________ to yours.
Ans. (i) accordance **(ii)** in comparison
(c) Use the following Phrasal verbs in sentence of your own:
look into
Ans. The CBI will now look into this case.
use up
Ans. I have used up all the sugars.
(d) Use the following words in two separate sentences to bring out the difference in their meaning:
minutes, Minutes
Ans. The programme lasted for 25 minutes.
I take care of every minute mistake.
(e) Write the antonyms of the following word and use them in meaningful sentences.
complicated, flexible
Ans. (i) Simple: This is a simple task. **(ii)** Rigid: Metals are rigid.

Q3. (a) Combine the following sentences into a single sentence using 'although':
(i) A menu-driven programme is easy to use.
(ii) At the same time it is not as powerful as the command driven programme.
Ans. A menu-driven programme is easy to use although it is not as powerful as the command driven programme at the same time.
(b) Complete the sentences using the correct form of verbs given in brackets:
(i) Many flyovers __________ (build) to ease the flow of traffic.
(ii) By the end of year 2009 India __________ (complete) most of the preparations for the Commonwealth Games.
Ans. (i) are being built
(ii) will have completed
(c) Combine the following sentences into a single sentence, using a relative clause.
The country cannot forget the day. A terrible storm hit one of its major cities that day.
Ans. The country cannot forget the day when its major cities were hit by a terrible storm.

Q4. Write a paragraph of about *150* words on any *one* of the following topic:
(a) The world has shrunk with advancement in communication
Ans. The Information Technology industry in India has been recording an annual average growth rate of 25% since July, 1991. Some of the biggest firms like Digital, Acer, Compaq, Dell and PH have set up manufacturing facilities and trading offices in India.
Large platform usage in India is restricted to big firms in the public sector and the private sector. The hardware market in India was estimated at $1 billion in 1994. Sales of PC's were just 180,000 which is a mere 1% of the total sales in the World. However, this figure is expected to touch the 1 million marks by the end of this century. Approximately 600,000 PC's are in use all over the country with nearly 20% of them connected in LANS. Most networking is in the Unix and Netware segments. The Unix segment serves primarily the CAD/ CAM and database users.
While PC's still dominate the hardware market, LAN server sales are growing at a fantastic rate. The growth rate in 1993-94 in the LAN server segment was a whopping 152%. The major customers for LAN's are the public sector units and the nationalized banks in India.
Indian computer companies have formed strategic alliances with major foreign players to meet the changing demand of Indian consumers. The country's biggest computer manufacturer. Hindustan Company Ltd. joined hands with

Hewlett-Packard to form HCL-HP. The second biggest firm in the country Wipro teamed up Acer of Taiwan.

The Indian strength in hardware is in design and integration of computers rather than manufacture of components. Peripherals such as keyboards, floppy drives, power supplies and printers are being manufactured in India.

India traditional strength has always been software because of the abundant availability of cheap and talented programmers. The software industry in India generated more than $600 million, most of it in exports, in 1993 and its growth over the last eight years has been more than 30% annually. A recent World Bank report estimates that Indian exports will touch $1 billion by the end of 1996. The biggest player in software is Tata Consultancy Services (TCS) owned by the Tata family which owns diverse interests from steel manufacturing to tea plantations. TCS employs about 4000 software professionals and has a clientele that includes JP Morgan and Prudential. The company had a turnover of $113 million in 1994 most of which was in exports.

Computer chip manufacturing is absent in India. About 50% of the chips in India are smuggled in from Singapore, Hong Kong and Taiwan. The duty on imported chips was reduced from 11% in 1993 to 61% in 1994. Despite the reduction the "grey market" as smuggled goods are known, continues to flourish. The Pentium chip costs about $1770 in India. Unless the import duty is brought to less than 10%, they grey market in India is going to flourish.

IT Usage: India has traditionally fought automation due to pro-labour policies followed by successive governments. The IT industry received its initial boost in 1986, when the government reduced duties on imported computer components. The computer manufacturing industry took off with many companies diversifying into assembling computers. Following the dismantling of the license system in 1991, foreign manufacturing companies started to invest into India.

The engine behind the growth of the IT industry in India has been software exports. This industry has been growing at an annual rate of 30% since 1988. There are no sings of abatement in that growth rate. There are an abundance of software programmers and skilled management personnel in India and this would attract more international companies to form tie-ups.

The customer base for hardware is split equally between the government and the private sector firms. The customer base transcends the type of industry. Embracing information technology is still slow in many government agencies, especially at the regional level. Though these agencies invest in computers, they do not use computers for anything else other than word processing. Many government agencies cannot hire computer professionals due to employment freezes.

Computers in India have a longer life period compared to developed countries. Due to the low cost of maintenance and high cost of new hardware, Indians tend to use computers for many years. The crucial advantage for India will be ability to leapfrog over many intermediate technologies and use the latest. The high cost of hardware forces programmers to develop cost effective and efficient programs that get the best out of the machines. Adaptability is an essential part of Indian culture. Hence there should not be any cultural factors that could inhibit the growth of information technology.

IT Strengths: India's strengths in the Information Technology arena are:

- Availability of unlimited pool of cheap and talented software personnel
- Presence of the biggest English speaking population after the United States
- Availability of western educated management personnel
- Lack of regulation in the software industry
- Burgeoning middle class of nearly 150 million consumers
- No baggage of outdated software technology
- Time difference advantage with countries like the United States

It manufacturing in India is going to be on the lines of assembling components manufactured in other countries. Since the import duty on hardware components is relatively high, there is a lot of smuggling of components from countries like Singapore and Taiwan into India. Most big Indian firms have formed strategic alliances with international companies like Hewlett-Packard and Acer. Hence investing in PC manufacturing is not expected produce immediate profits. However the LAN and the peripheral markets are growing at fantastic rates and could be good investment areas for companies, which are looking to invest in overseas IT manufacturing.

Based on the software export growth in India, offshore programming ventures will continue to remain profitable for the next few years. The threats India could face in this area are from Philippines and Pakistan, both of which like India have a large pool of trained IT personnel.

IT Weaknesses: India's biggest weakness would be in the area of telecommunication infrastructure. India's telecommunication infrastructure is poor compared even to developing countries. The reason behind this has been the state monopoly over telecommunication in India.

Most public sector agencies have become white elephants. Until recently, Indian politicians were hesitant to antagonize the powerful labour unions of the state run telecommunication agencies. In 1994, there were half hearted attempts to sell some of the shares in these firms. The employees promptly went on strike. The government has taken a bold step in allowing private competition to the Department of Telecommunication (DoT). In order for India to become a strong player in the IT market, the government has to dismantle bureaucratic controls which discourage foreign firms from investing in India.

The lack of infrastructure forces companies to invest on high cost items like satellite links and high-speed lines. Not all firms would be able to afford such capital costs both in terms of money and time. This cost could be a major restraint for the IT industry.

The government has to become a major customer for the IT industry to encourage the growth of the domestic software and hardware industry. At present there is a great deal of resistance in government circles against investing in computers.

Impact on the (non-IT) globally competing firm: Following the liberalization era, which began in 1991, India became one of the big emerging markets. At the same time the government realizing the importance of information technology started reducing the import duties and excise taxes on fax machines and computers. Prior to this, these items were considered a luxury and taxed at the highest possible rate.

Suddenly computers became affordable to not only businesses but the average middle class consumer as well. As the sale of computers grew, there was a whole industry built around technical support for software and hardware. The availability of a vast resource of technical personnel made it a buyer's market in terms of competitive pricing.

One of the most important changes has been the recognition of the computer as a valuable management tool. Today computers are viewed as a necessity by most firms irrespective of their size. Personnel turnover is still a major problem faced by Indian industries. Some industries are insisting on new recruits to sign employment contracts with them. Salaries in most of the firms for IT professionals are still low because of the abundant availability.

The computer revolution has finally hit India. The impact on the globally competing firm irrespective whether it is an International firm or an Indian firm remains to be seen.

(b) Computers have brought in both speed and efficiency in our day to day functioning

Refer to Page No.-186 to 188

(c) A clean environment is both a healthy and a happy environment

Refer to Page No.-139 to 140

Q5. Write an essay of about *300* words on any *one* of the following:

(a) Advantages and disadvantages of e-courses

Ans. More and more young people are becoming attracted to the idea of e-courses. Many believe that signing up with accredited institutions for perfectly legitimate diplomas will give them the time and space they need to do other things.

The advantages and disadvantages of e-courses vary greatly between institutions. Some institutions that offer distance learning offer very comprehensive curriculums, which may be a boon particularly for young people who wish to study and work full-time; they may set their research and composition time after regular working hours, so they could better feel that they are in control of their time.

Working at home could be quite taxing, especially if you already have a family and are looking after an entire household. The distractions abound. One needs enormous discipline and energy in order to study for a correspondence degree course while at home, especially if one is also working full-time.

Also, one should not think that just because a course is online, a student may be spared lab work, legwork for research, one-on-one consultations with the professor, group meetings with classmates and other regular classroom requirements.

One empirical disadvantage that may arise is the difficulty of transferring credits from an e-course to an existing or future study program. Not all universities accept e-class credits for certain courses, and some universities even have strict rules as to which exercises they will and will not credit. Before signing up for an e-course, map out your academic plans carefully. Have a clear idea where you want to proceed after you have finished the online course, and what you plan to use your distance education degree for. Coordinate with the necessary institutions to make sure your performance at an e-class will be credited. This knowledge will help you become more accurate in determining the advantages and disadvantages of e-courses of your choice.

(b) Net working through computers

Ans. Computer Networking is the practice of linking two or more computers together for the purpose of sharing data. Networks are built with a mix of computer hardware and computer software.

Area Networks: Networks can be categorized in several different ways. One approach defines the type of network according to the geographic area it spans. Local area networks (LANs), for example, typically reach across a single home, whereas wide area networks (WANs), reach across cities, states, or even across the world. The Internet is the world's largest public WAN.

Network Design: Computer networks also differ in their design. The two types of high-level network design are called client-server and peer-to-peer. Client-server networks feature centralized server computers that store email, Web pages, files and or applications. On a peer-to-peer network, conversely, all computers tend to support the same functions. Client-server networks are much more common in business and peer-to-peer networks much more common in homes.

A network topology represents its layout or structure from the point of view of data flow. In so-called bus networks, for example, all of the computers share and communicate across one common conduit, whereas in a star network, all data flows through one centralized device. Common types of network topologies include bus, star, ring and mesh.

Network Protocols: In networking, the communication language used by computer devices is called the protocol. Yet another way to classify computer networks is by the set of protocols they support. Networks often implement multiple protocols to support specific applications. Popular protocols include TCP/IP, the most common protocol found on the Internet and in home networks.

Wired vs. Wireless Networking: Many of the same network protocols, like TCP/IP, work in both wired and wireless networks. Networks with Ethernet cables predominated in businesses, schools, and homes for several decades. Recently, however, wireless networking alternatives have emerged as the premier technology for building new computer networks.

A situation that may arise in homes where there is only one computer occurs when you have a rush assignment or presentation and you can't get on the computer. This situation is still a reality for some people. The employer did not provide a computer and there is only one in the house. When you have to fight for time in the evenings or on weekends at the computer, what is the solution? For too many people the only option they have at this time is to get in their vehicle and drive to the office to get the work done. This solution of course defeats the purpose of working remotely.

•One of the best advantages to networking your home PC's is that you can share printers and other peripherals between the networked units. There is no need to buy extra peripherals or go through the hassle of disconnecting and re-connecting peripherals and moving them around.

•Most networking solutions you can share Internet access. That alone is well worth the investment of a home office network.

•You can also share applications across the network and share the hard drive resources. In this respect you don't need to have two PC's with huge hard drives to handle the workloads. You can even run a lower end PC using the resources of your other PC.

•Another benefit of having your own home network is when you have a project that you are completing with a co-worker:

They can come to your location and you could work together this way. There would be fewer distractions and the project could possibly be completed in a more timely fashion. This would be a really good option, especially if you are not on a network from your work. It could save a lot of phone calls, emails and even trips back and for the to office.

(c) Computer in industry vs. the labour-force

Ans. Nothing epitomizes modern life better than the computer. For better or worse, computers have infiltrated every aspects of our society. Today computers do much more than simply compute, supermarket scanners calculate our grocery bill while keeping store inventory; computerized telephone switching centers play traffic cop to millions of cells and keep lines of communication untangled and automatic teller machines (ATM) let us conduct banking transactions from virtually anywhere in the World. But where did all this technology come from and where is it heading? To fully understand and appreciate the impact computers have on our lives and promises they hold for the future, it is important to understand their evolution.

The history of computers starts out about 2000 years ago, at the birth of the **Abacus**, a wooden rack holding two horizontal wires with beads strung on them. When these beads are moved around, according to programming rules memorized by the user, all regular arithmetic problems can be done. Another important invention around the same time was the **Astrolabe**, used for navigation. Blaise Pascal is usually credited for building the first **digital** computer in 1642. It added numbers entered with dails and was made to help his father, a tax collector. In 1671, Gottfried Wilhelm von Leibniz invented a computer that was built in 1694. It could add and after changing some things around, multiply. Leibniz invented a computer that was built in 1694. It could add and after changing some things around, multiply. Leibniz invented a special **stepped gear mechanism** for introducing the addend digits and this is still being used. The prototypes made by Pascal and Leibniz were not used in many places and considered weird until a little more than a century later, when Thomas of Colmar created the first successful mechanical calculator that could add, subtract, multiply and divide. A lot of improved desktop calculators by many inventors followed, so that by about 1890, the range of improvements such as Accumulation of partial results; Storage and automatic reentry of past results and Printing of the results were included. But each of these required manual installation. These improvements were mainly made for commercial users and not for the needs of science.

While Thomas of Colmar was developing the desktop calculator a series of very interesting developments in computers was started in Cambridge, England, by Charles Babbage, a mathematics professor. In 1812, Babbage realized that many long calculations, especially those needed to make mathematical tables, were really a series of predictable actions that were constantly repeated. From this he suspected that it should be possible to do these automatically.

He began to design an automatic mechanical calculating machine in 1822, which the called a difference engine. The difference engine, although having limited adaptability and applicability, was really a great advance. Babbage continued to work on if for the next 10 years, but in 1833 he lost interest because he thought he had a **better idea** the construction of what would now be called a general purpose, fully program controlled, automatic mechanical digital computer.

The plans for this engine required an identical decimal computer operating on numbers of 50 decimal digits and having a storage capacity of 1,000 such digits. The built-in operations were supposed to include everything that a modern general purpose computer would need, even the all important **Conditional Control Transfer Capability** that would allow commands to be executed in any order, not just the order in which they were programmed.

The computer development was grown on year by year by the works of many brilliants. The saturation level of computer was reached after one and half centuries i.e., in 1981, IBM introduced its personal computer (PC) for use in the home, office and schools. The 1980's saw an expansion in computer use in all three arenas as clones of the IBM PC made the personal computer even more affordable. The numbers of personal computers in use more than doubled from 2 million in 1981 to 5.5 million in 1982. Ten years later, 65 million PCs were being used. Computer continued their trend toward a smaller size, working their way down from desktop to laptop computers, which could fit inside a briefcase to palmtop, able to fit inside a breast pocket. In direct competition with IBM's PC was Apple's Macintosh line, introduced in 1984. Notable for its user-friendly design, the Macintosh offered an operating system that allowed users to move screen icons instead of typing instructions. Users controlled the screen cursor using a mouse, a device that mimicked the movement of one's hand on the computer screen.

As computer became more widespread in the workplace, new ways to harness their potential developed. As smaller computers became more powerful, they could be linked together or networked, to share memory space, software and information and communicate with each other. As opposed to a mainframe computer, which was one powerful computer that shared time with many terminals for many applications, networked computers allowed individual computers to form electronic co-ops. Using either direct wiring, called a Local Area Network (LAN) or telephone lines, these networks could reach enormous proportions. A global web of computer circuitry, the Internet, for example, links computers worldwide into a single network of information.

Q6. Read the following passage and summarise it to one third of its length; give a suitable title as well also.

Global warming is the theorized increase in the average measured temperature of the Earth's near-surface air and oceans since the mid-20th century and its projected continuation.

The average global air temperature near the Earth's surface increased $0.74 \pm 0.18°C$ (between $56°C$ and $92°C$) during the 100 years ending in 2005. The Intergovernmental Panel on Climate Change (IPCC) concludes that most of the observed increase in globally averaged temperatures since the mid-twentieth century is very likely due to the observed increase in man-made greenhouse gas concentrations through an enhanced greenhouse effect. Natural phenomena such as solar variation combined with volcanoes probably had a small warming effect from pre-industrial times to 1950 and a small cooling effect from 1950 onward.

Though some individual scientists have voiced disagreement with some findings of the IPCC, the overwhelming majority of scientists and at least 30 scientific communities and academics of science of major industrialized countries, working on climate change agree with the IPCC's main conclusions.

Climate model projections summarized by the IPCC indicate that average global surface temperature will likely rise a further 1.1 to $6.4°C$ during the twenty-first century. This range of values results from the use of

differing scenarios of future greenhouse gas emissions as well as models with differing climate sensitivity. Although most studies focus on the period up to 2100, warming and sea level rise are expected to continue for more than a thousand years even if green house gas levels are stabilized. The delay in reaching equilibrium is a result of the large heat capacity of the oceans.

Increasing global temperature is expected to cause sea level to rise, an increase in the intensity of extreme weather events and significant changes to the amount and pattern of precipitation, likely leading to an expanse of tropical areas and increased pace of decertification. Other expected effects of global warming include changes in agricultural yields, modifications of trade routes, glacier retreat, species extinctions and increases in the ranges of disease vectors.

Remaining scientific uncertainties include the amount of warming expected in the future and how warming and related changes will vary from region to region around the globe. Most national governments have signed and ratified the Kyoto Protocol aimed at reducing greenhouse gas emissions, but there is an ongoing political and public debate worldwide regarding what, if any, action should be taken to reduce or reverse future warming or to adapt to its expected consequences.

Ans. Global warming has been measured since the mid 20th century with the average changes in the earth's surface, near air and ocean temperatures. In 2005 there was an increase of about $0.18°C$. The global increase in temperature is due to the emission of greenhouse gases. There has been noted a continuous temperature change from the pre industrialized period to 1950 and from 1950 to now. Most of the world's scientists and many other scientific organizations agree with the IPCC's main coalitions about the reasons and effects of global warming. It say by 21st century, the temperature will rise upto $64°C$. Most studies are centered with the 2100 and believe though the green house gases be stable the sea level will continue to rise due to the heat effect. This increase in sea level may cause changes in weather conditions like precipitations. The agricultural yields can also change, glaciers will retreat and trade routes will also have to change. Studies have also been done to know the variations of effect on various places on the earth. The Kyoto protocol was made to reduce the emissions of greenhouse gases. And there is a continuous worldwide public debate going on this topic.

Title: Global Warming Solutions

CS–610: FOUNDATION COURSE IN ENGLISH FOR COMPUTING
December, 2009

*Note: Attempt **all** the questions.*

Q1. Read the passage and answer the questions that follow:

It had not rained, for the dust which arose beneath the man's feet had a horrible damp stickiness. His face and hands were grimy, as were his sheets, his cheap, ready-made suit, and his straw hat. However, the man felt a pride in his clothes, for they were at least the garb of freedom. He had come out of prison the day before, and had scorned the suit provided to him by the officials. He had given it away, and bought a new one with a good part of the small stock of money that he had.

This suit was of a small checked pattern. Looking at it, nobody could tell, that the wearer had just left jail. He had been there for several years for one of the minor offences against the law. His term would probably have been shorter, but the judge had been careless, and he had no friends. Stebbins had never been the sort to make many friends although he had never cherished animosity towards any human being. Even some injustice in his sentence had not caused him to feel any rancour.

During his stay in the prison he had not been really unhappy. He had accepted the inevitable-the yoke of the strong for the weak-with a patience which brought almost a sense of enjoyment.

(a) Why did Stebbins discard the suit offered by the jail officials?

Ans. Stebbins discarded the suit offered by the jail officials because it was similar to the Jail suits (uniform) and he did not want others to know that he had come out of the jail.

(b) Do you think Stebbins suffered more than he should have? Pick sentences from the passage in support of your answer.

Ans. Yes, he did suffer more than required. The sentence which tells us this is.... "His term would probably have been shorter, but the judge had been careless, and he had no friends".

(c) Was he able to accept this situation with equanimity? Pick a sentence from the passage to illustrate your answer.

Ans. Yes, he wasn't very unhappy or discontented about the situation. the sentence that tells us this is.... "He had accepted the inevitable-the Yoke of the strong for the weak- with a patience which brought almost a sense of enjoyment".

(d) From the passage pick words/phrases that mean the following:
(i) he had no anger or hatred towards anyone.
Ans. Never cherished animosity towards any human being

(ii) the power of the strong over the weak
Ans. 'the Yoke of the strong for the weak'

(e) What might have happened if he would have had some friends?
Ans. His jail term would have probably been short, if he had some friends.

(f) Write the antonyms of the following:
grimy, minor
Ans. Grimy: Clean, cheerful, **Minor:** Major; Adult

(g) Explain these phrases from the passage:
(i) garb of freedom
Ans. He appearance showed that as he was a free man the feeling of being set free is being talked about here..

(ii) a goodly part of…
Ans. Major portion of (his money).

(iii) accepted the inevitable
Ans. Acceptance of what is unavoidable.

(iv) almost a sense of enjoyment
Ans. Reaching a sense of enjoyment and acceptance as there was no other alternative, without actually enjoying.

Q2. Correct the following sentences:
(a) (i) many expeditions have been undertaken in Himalayas.
Ans. Many expeditions have been undertaken in the Himalayas

(ii) I read his biography because I needed finding out the truth about his life
Ans. I read his biography because I needed to find out
the truth about his life.

(b) Fill in the blanks with appropriate model.

(i) We_________do something about the sagging roof of our tent.

Ans. need to

(ii) _______If___you meet the Asst. Manger on the way, ———— you ask him to meet me.

Ans. can

(c) Use the following phrasal verbs into sentences of your own.

get by, take after

Ans. Get by: We'll get by if we economize.

Take after: She takes after her mother.

(d) Use the following words in two separate sentences to bring out the difference in their meaning.

Accede, exceed.

Ans. Accede: The prince acceded to the throne.

Exceed : The river exceeded its banks.

(e) Write the antonyms of the following words and use them (antonyms) in meaningful sentences.

ancient, complete.

Ans. Ancient : Modern: He maintains a modern lifestyle.

Complete : Incomplete The answer was incomplete

Q3. (a) Combine the following sentences into a single sentence using 'not only-but also'

(i) Today computers are affordable.

(ii) In addition they are user friendly.

Ans. Today computers are not only affordable but also user friendly.

(b) Combine the following sentences using a relative clause:

(i) posters were put up in the market place.

(ii) everyone could see them there

Ans. The posters were put up in the market place, so that everyone could see them there.

(c) Fill in the blanks with the correct form of tense of the verb given in brackets:

(i) If it beings to rain the match___________(abandon).

Ans. will be abandoned

(ii) If we___________ (take) adequate measures to curb global warming, the glaciers would not have melted.
Ans. had taken

Q4. Write a paragraph of about 150 words on any one of the following:
(a) The effect of computers on the human brain.
Ans. Refer to Dec-2006, Q.No.-6(iii), Page No.-163
Also Refer to June-2004, Q.No.-5(b), Page No.-83

(b) The importance of English in today's world.
Ans. Refer to June-2008, Q.No.-4(i), P-183

(c) The impact of e-mails and short messaging systems.
Ans. E-mails : Refer to June-2005, Q.No.-6(ii), Page No.-56
Also Refer to June-2003, Q.No.-5(a), Page No.-82
SMS:
SMS-short message service is an application by the mobile provider to send messages anywhere, anytime and to anyone. As mobile has become a need more than a luxury in our day-to-day life, it's become more and more easier to stay in touch and communicate, and to keep oneself abreast of the changes in the dynamics of the world. As a professional, we often feel a greater comfort level with the digital media nowadays. We need to take some basic steps to help ourselves become more knowledgeable and avoid inconvenience due to non acquaintance with SMS. For those not working with mobile on a daily basis and looking for ways to communicate with their friends SMS is a very a economical option. It costs one tenth of a Phone call and gets instant response. It is extremely convenient, affordable and accessible also. in the midst of a meeting or an emergency. it comes as a rescue. and not to forget it links people and is a mode of social networking too.

Q5. Write an essay of about 300 words on any one of the following:
(a) Cyber crime
Ans. Refer to Dec-2005, Q.No.-4(i), Page No.-143

(b) Computers have ushered in both speed and efficiency in different fields.
Ans. Refer to Jun-2008, Q-5(iii), Page No.-186

(c) Advantages and disadvantages of e-courses.
Ans. Refer to June-2009, Q.No.-5(a), Page No.-199

Q6. Read the following passage and summarize it to one-third of its length: Give it a suitable title.

(Passage for summarization)

There are many myths surrounding the origin of the ancient Olympic Games, the most popular of which identifies Heracles as the creator of the Olympic Games. According to the legend, Heracles built the Olympic stadium and surrounding building as an honour to his father Zeus. After he built the stadium he walked in a straight line for 400 strides and called this distance a "stadion" (Latin: stadium, "stage") that late also became a unit of distance. This is also why a modern stadium track is 400 meters in circumference-the distance a runner travels in one lap (1 stadium =400m). Another myth associates the first Games with the ancient Greak concept of ekecheiria, Olympic truce. The date of the Games' creation was based on a four year cycle. The most widely held estimate for the inception of the Ancient Olympics is 776 BC.

From then on, the Olympic Games quickly became much more important throughout ancient Greece, reaching their zenith in the 6th and 5th centuries BC. The Olympics were of fundamental religious importance, contests alternating with sacrifices and ceremonies honouring both Zeus (colossal statue stood at Olympia), and Pelops, divine hero and mythical king of Olympia, who was famous for his legendary chariot races. The number of events increased to twenty, and the celebration was spread over several days. Winners of the events were greatly admired and were immortalized in poems and statues. The Games were held every four years, and the period between two celebrations became known as an Olympiad. The Greeks used Olympiads as one of their units of time measurement. The most famous Ancient Olympic athlete lived during the sixth century BC: the wrestler Milo of Croton is the athlete in history to win a victory in six Olympics.

The Games gradually declined in importance as the Romans gained power in Greece. After Emperor Theodosius I proclaimed Christianity the religion of the Empire in AD 393 and banned pagan rites, the Olympic Games were outlawed as pagan festival. The Olympics were not seen again until their rebirth 1,500 years later.

Ans. Title: History of the Olympics

There are many myths surrounding the origin of the ancient Olympic Games, The moist popular which identifies Heracles as the creator of the Olympic Games. According to the legend, Heracles built the Olympic stadium and surrounding buildings as an honour to his father Zeus. From then on, the Olympic Games quickly became much more important throughout ancient Greece, reaching their zenith in the 6th and 5th centuries BC. The most widely held estimate for the inception of the Ancient Olympic is 776 BC. After Emperor Theodosius I proclaimed Christianity the religion of the Empire in AD 393 and banned pagan rites, the Olympic Games were outlawed as a pagan festival and were not seen again until their rebirth 1,500 years later.

CS–610: FOUNDATION COURSE IN ENGLISH FOR COMPUTING
June, 2010

Note: Attempt ***all*** *the questions.*

Q1. Read the passage given below and answer the question that follows it.

'A great mass' of something means a great amount. When the new method of manufacturing articles in great numbers was introduced, a new name was required for it and 'Mass production' was the one that come into use.

In what ways does mass production differ from the older methods of manufacturing? Formerly a craftsman, or skilled workman, often made the whole of an article himself by hand. He put into his work all his skill, all his experience. He was proud of the fruits of his labour. His reputation, his standing among his fellows, depended on his skill and on his character. He would have been ashamed if any serious fault had appeared in his work. He was envied and admired by fellow-craftsmen whose skill was not equal to his own. Articles made in this way could not be mass-produced. Each article differed slightly from the others; in every one there was something of the maker's individuality. The finished article was sold at a high price, the price representing the time and the skill of the craftsman who had made it.

Many such articles, made long ago with loving care, possess a quality and a beauty that mass-produced goods cannot equal. The wonderful pottery of ancient China, the lovely carpets of Persia, the engraved sword of Damascus, the silver-ware of the Middle Ages-all these things show the individual craftsmanship of their long-dead makers.

(a) Say whether the following statements are true (T) of false (F) :

(i) The term 'Mass Production' means a unique method of manufacturing goods.

Ans. True

(ii) The articles manufactured on a mass scale are cheaper than the ones made by skilled workers single handedly.

Ans. True

(b) Explain the phrases 'fruits of his labour' and 'long-dead makers'.
Ans. Fruits of labour: This phrase here refers to the end product, i.e. the result that has been made after the skilled craftsmen has put in his hardwork and time and energy into it.
Long dead makers: It here refers to the artisans or the craftsmen who used to make such handmade unique products.

(c) Pick out from the passage, four examples of things were not the result of mass production. What is special about them?
Ans. The wonderful pottery of ancient China, the lovely carpets of Persia, the engraved sword of Damascus, the silver-ware of the Middle Ages. The specialty of these items lies in their uniqueness, creativity and originality, that gives the distinctive style of the craftsmen to each product.

(d) Pick out words from the passage which have the same meaning as the following words :
fame, artisan.
Ans. fame: reputation, **artisan:** craftsman

Q2. (a) Rewrite the following sentences in passive voice :
(i) Shut the door.
Ans. Let the door be shut.

(ii) The chairman presented a comprehensive report of the company's working.
Ans. A comprehensive report of the company's working was provided by the chairman.

(b) Fill in the blanks with suitable options from the ones given in brackets:
(i) When I was young I___________(use to, used to) go to school on foot.
Ans. used to

(ii) I__________(have, am having) two books on modern art.
Ans. have

(iii) Modern technology__________(was, is) a great blessing for us.
Ans. is

Q3. Rewrite the following sentences removing the errors, if any :
(a) Our class starts by 10 a.m. sharp.
Ans. Our class starts by sharp 10a.m.

(b) I cannot cope up with the stress of modern life.
Ans. I cannot cope with the stress of modern life.

(c) Though he wrote pages after pages, he could not score well.
Ans. Though he wrote pages after pages, still he could not score well.

(d) Yesterday I had gone to visit the Book Fair.
Ans. Correct

(e) He was promoted to the post of Principal though he was junior than many others.
Ans. He was promoted to the post of Principal though he was junior to many others.

Q4. Do as directed :
(a) Computers are a boon of modern technology (add a question tag)
Ans. Computers are a boon of modern technology. Aren't they?

(b) Combine and rewrite the following sentences as a single sentence. Do *not* use *and* or *but*.
(i) It rained heavily in Kolkata
(ii) Life went on a usual
Ans. Although it rained heavily in Calcutta, life went on as usual.

(c) He said to me, "Will you go to the market tomorrow?"
(Change into indirect speech)
Ans. He asked me if I would go to the market the next day.

(d) Give the antonyms of the following words :
Victory, active
Ans. Victory – defeat, **Active** – passive

(e) Use the following words in sentences of your own in order to bring out their meaning :
lubricant, luxurious
Ans. Lubricants are used to make the machinery running smoothly.
A luxurious life style is yearned by all.

Q5. Write a composition in about 300 words, on any one of the following topics.
(a) Technology classrooms in the twenty second century.
(b) The world as a global village

(c) Protect the environment for the sake of coming generations.

Ans. (c) The environment and our mother earth is suffering and infact bleeding because of the atocities of humans have been selfish and have not shown any gratitude towards the mother earth. The depletion of natural resources and so many occurrences of natural disasters are all a result of the human activity. With the advent of technology and machines, although life has become easy, but even humans have become mechanical. We need to save this for the coming generations, as they are going to be the real sufferers. It is important to encourage plantation of trees and so many other activities to protect the environment for future.

Q6. Summarize the following passage in about 100-150 words and give it an appropriate title.

It is difficult to find a newspaper or magazine throughout the world which during the past few years had not published material on the severe damage which man inflicts on his environment, i.e., on the Earth's biosphere. It may appear that the public response to the ever-increasing pollution of soil, water and air has already exceeded, in scale, the problem itself. Probably during the entire existence of civilization no other problem has evoked such keen and, literally speaking, universal interest, such far-reaching and at times diametrically opposite opinions.

Professor Meadows, USA, is of the opinion that if the present growth of the population, industrialization, environmental pollution and the plunder of natural resources continue on the same scale, then the absolute limit of growth on earth will be exceeded within the coming 100 years. This would lead to a rather rapid and unrestrained drop in the size of population and production.

A British author holds quite a different point of view. He claims that the nature protection movement has caused more harm than good. The danger is not of a greater menace that those which had confronted mankind in the past. Typhus and cholera, these terrible disasters of the past, have practically disappeared in Western Europe. Diphtheria and tuberculosis have become rare. Do not these examples from history provide ground for hoping that the highly developed countries will succeed in coping, rationally and in good time, with the pollution of nature which today horrifies us?

Ans. Summary

It is difficult to find a newspaper or magazine throughout the world which during the past few years had not published material on the severe damage which man inflicts on his environment, i.e., on the Earth's biosphere. Everywhere around such related topics are the talks of the town. Professor

Meadows, USA, is of the opinion that if the present growth of the population, industrialization, environmental pollution and the plunder of natural resources continue on the same scale, then the absolute limit of growth on earth will be exceeded within the coming 100 years. This would lead to a rather rapid and unrestrained drop in the size of population and production.

A British author holds quite a different point of view. Typhus and cholera, Diphtheria and tuberculosis have become rare. These examples from history provide ground for hoping that the highly developed countries will succeed in coping, rationally and in good time, with the pollution of nature which today horrifies us?